LOVELY things

TO MAKE

for GIRLS of Slender Means

LOVELY things

TO MAKE

for GIRLS of Slender Means

EITHNE FARRY

W&N

First published in Great Britain in 2010 by Weidenfeld & Nicolson
An imprint of the Orion Publishing Group Ltd
Orion House, 5 Upper St Martin's Lane
London WC2H 9EA

An Hachette UK Company
1 3 5 7 9 10 8 6 4 2

ISBN 978 0 297 85954 3

Design and illustration: Laura Brett & www.carrstudio.co.uk
Photography: Guiliana Casserotti
Printed and bound in Spain

Excerpt from *The Girls of Slender Means* by Muriel Spark reproduced
with the kind permission of Penguin.

www.orionbooks.co.uk

CONTENTS

SPRING

SUMMER

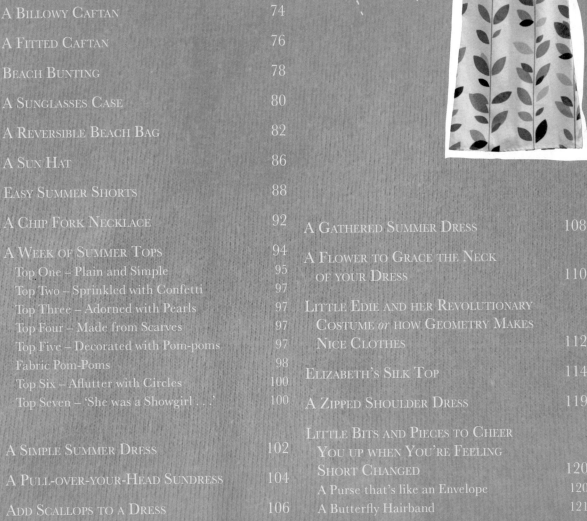

AUTUMN

WINTER

Champagne tastes

LEMONADE
BUDGET

He said, 'I don't think I've ever
seen such a gorgeous dress.'

'Schiaparelli,' she said.

He said, 'Is that the one you swap
amongst yourselves?'

'Who told you that?'

'You look beautiful,' he replied.

She picked up the rustling skirts and
floated away up the staircase.

Oh, girls of Slender means!

'The Girls of Slender Means' by MURIEL SPARK, 1963

9

INTRODUCTION

I often wish I had an aristocratic aunt with a wardrobe crammed full of heirloom clothes. She'd sail out to a swishy cocktail party, wearing a beautiful beaded dress, drink something lovely from a fluted glass, and then the next morning she'd hand over the frock to me. I don't have a rich relative, but some of my favourite clothes are cast-offs, foraged from charity shops. My best dress originally came from a New York boutique, but I acquired it in South London. Designed by Molly Parniss, it's black chiffon with a beautifully pleated skirt – the sort of dress that an Irish widow might wear to the funeral of her husband, whose death she had a hand in.

My prettiest shirt is a treasured Liberty-print one where the cotton is worn to softness and fragility. Again, it's a charity shop purchase, but I adapted it. I shortened the sleeves so that they are three-quarter length and kept the cuffs for bracelets. When I wear it, it looks like part of the shirt has mysteriously disappeared, in a magic trick gone wrong. The fabric is thin now, fraying and coming apart at the seams, even though I carefully repair it every time it rips. I don't mind my clothes looking a little worn. At the local vintage fair my favourite stall is the one where the flapper frocks are dropping their sequins like splashes of moonlight, and the tea dresses have small tears in the chiffon – they haven't been stored away unworn for years, but shimmied into for nights of dancing.

I have a dream dress in my head. It is dark blue, crisp cotton, with 'shower of hail' white spots sprinkled all over it. It has a fitted bodice top, with a row of buttons around the neck and a zip at the back to fasten it. It has a huge circle skirt, with an underskirt made of navy blue tulle. I'd like to think, if I really had this dress I'd take good care of it. But I know what would really happen. I'd almost immediately forget all my good intentions, and find myself heading backwards down a helter skelter in it – a big mistake, resulting in instant disorientation, and me crashing into a group of picnickers and squashing their sandwiches. And then I'd probably go for a paddle in a choppy South-East coast sea, ending up with a salt lick on the hem of the skirt. I'd wear the dress out dancing and bowling, drinking and singing, until it was thoroughly bedraggled, and pretty much unwearable despite being repaired over and over again. I wouldn't be able to bear throwing it away, so what I'd do was set about making it into something else:

- The sleeves could become spotted corsages, threaded with sequins

- The buttons could be added to the button jar, ready to be turned into a cascading button decoration

- The zip could be saved and put on a new dress

- The top of the dress could be turned into a lining fabric for a bag, and the full-circle, slightly torn skirt, sewn into an apron

- The tulle could be snipped into a delicate evening wrap decorated with velvet bows, haphazardly sewn like a flurry of moths

- And anything else that was left over and was of a fair size could migrate to the patchwork pile; and the last scrappy remnants would be perfect to make fabric beads on a delicate pleated necklace.

My second dream dress is a more whimsical wish. It's a dress of spring and summer, bedecked with living sweet peas, which send out tendrils of growth, until there is a cascade of scented blooms draped around the neck and shoulders . . .

And that's the spirit of *Lovely Things to Make for Girls of Slender Means*. Having champagne tastes and a lemonade budget does not mean embracing a life of dowdy drabness; instead it's a chance to get creative: you can be prettily practical, sweetly silly, wildly inventive. All you need is a bit of imagination and some simple DIY skills.

Lovely Things to Make for Girls of Slender Means is all about being inventive and resourceful with the clothes you already own – having fun with buttons and sequins and velvety ribbons that don't cost much but can make a plain dress fancy. Or sewing something from scratch with two hundred centimetres of lovely fabric. Trust me, nothing can beat that glowy sense of accomplishment when you skip the light fantastic in a frock that you've made yourself.

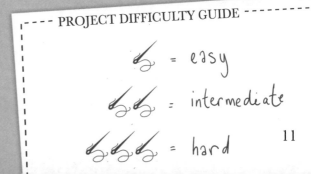

PROJECT DIFFICULTY GUIDE

✂ = easy

✂✂ = intermediate

✂✂✂ = hard

11

BEFORE you stART

You don't have to have tons of technical equipment to start making things. The little list below spells out the essentials. And adds a few fripperies to your sewing vocabulary.

Sewing Stuff

What you need to get started ...

A REALLY GOOD PAIR OF DRESSMAKER'S SCISSORS. Don't skimp on these, cutting fabric with a good blade is a snippy joy; a blunt blade will result in raggedy edges and frustration. The golden rule is: only use your dressmaking scissors to cut fabric, cutting hair, paper or old bits of carpet will wreck them. (Cutting up an old carpet with scissors will also wreck your fingers and thumb.)

A SMALL PAIR OF SCISSORS for cutting paper, bits of ribbon, birds' nests of thread and the like.

PINKING SHEARS. Not essential, but their toothy blades cut a nice zigzag edge which prevents (or delays) fraying on fabric and adds a decorative touch to felt.

I also have a lovely, little pair of scissors in the shape of a heron, which I don't use very often, but like seeing in my sewing tin.

PINS. Lots of them. I am forever pinning dresses together, trying them on and then leaving a silver pathway of shiny metal behind me. I'm tempted to buy a giant magnet and retrace my route from mirror to sewing machine; the magnet would bristle like an angry porcupine with dropped pin spines.

A PIN TIN OR A PINCUSHION. I keep a pile of pins in an old sweet tin, and my pincushion is a patchwork flower. I especially love the idea of sailors' pincushions. On long sea voyages, they made keepsakes for their land-bound sweethearts, spelling out tender messages – 'dear heart' and 'forget me not' in a glint of pins. My cushiony exhortation? 'Get a grip lady.' (And for men, simply add a 'd'.)

HAND-SEWING NEEDLES. For tacking, appliquéing or mending a bedraggled hem. Buy a multipack and that'll cover all eventualities.

THREAD. Ideally, the type of thread you use should be the same as the fabric you've gone for – cotton thread for natural fibres, polyester for man-made fibres, silk for silk. And choose an ever-so-slightly darker shade than your material, that way your stitches will blend in nicely.

A TAPE MEASURE, vital for working out your vital statistics, but also handy for measuring curves and corners on fabric.

A RULER. I quite like a transparent one.

TAILOR'S CHALK, in white and blue. Use the white chalk for marking dark fabrics and the blue on everything else. Chalk wipes away with a swipe of the hand, unlike felt pen, biro, charcoal. When I first started sewing, I grabbed the first that came to hand, thinking that big bold lines would be easy to follow. And they were, but the big bold marks didn't wash out, and some days my clothes looked like road maps.

A SEAM RIPPER (AKA A QUICK UNPICK). When things go to hell in a handcart on the sewing front this handy little thing will unpick askew stitches, take apart awry seams and undo higgledy-piggledy hems. I have three of them.

AN IRON, with a good steam function. It really, really does make a difference. Fabric will be crease free, wonky stitches will become straight, and hems and seams will be crisp and even.

A SEWING MACHINE. I like to hand-sew stuff sometimes – a bit of patchworking while watching *Murder She Wrote*, an hour of backstitching a *coup de foudre* motto to the hem of a little black dress, but my sewing machine is my most essential thing. As I said in *Yeah I Made It Myself*: DON'T FEAR THE SEWING MACHINE . . . Initially the thought of using one might make you shivery with horror, but once you get to grips with the basics you'll be whizzing up beach bags, summer dresses and autumn capelets with a studied insouciance. Honestly.

As this is your biggest investment it's worth doing a bit of research before you hand over your cash. Consult friends who are machine savvy, try out different models in your local sewing centre or department store and see what suits. It may be tempting to go for a top-of-the-range model, but I recently bought a new machine (the one I've had for years and years finally gave up the ghost) for about £200 and it does everything I need and more, and I still haven't used half the functions or stitches on it.

Once you've bought the machine, read the manual (a bit boring, but all the tech talk is necessary and truly illuminating). Prop it next to the machine and work your way through all the essentials, from learning to thread up the machine, to trying out all the stitches, to learning how to troubleshoot when things go off kilter. Have some scrappy bits of fabric on hand to practise your newly acquired skills, and then try a simple project – like the apron on page 46 or the caftan on page 74.

Other useful things to add to your sewing kit

BUTTONS. Salvaged from old cardis, snipped from coats, foraged from charity shops and purchased in hushed haberdashery shops as a treat, stored in a big button jar, and sewed onto anything that needs some decorative detail.

BIAS BINDING. Another one of my favourite things. It's a strip of fabric that's used to give a neat look to a raw edge. It comes in a rainbow of colours, and because it's cut on the bias, it curves nicely so that you can sew it just as easily around necks and armholes as along a straight hem or a jaunty side seam.

BRAID, RIBBON, SEQUINS. Treats! Bold braid can be added to the necks of tunics, the cuffs of sleeves, or made into a hasty belt; use the ribbon for ties for decorative collars and pom-pom necklaces or work them into tiny bows to decorate plain hair slides. Sequins! If I could buy them by the lb I would, especially big disco-style paillettes. You can never have too much plastic fantastic sparkle.

INTERFACING. This is a special kind of fabric that adds strength, shape and structure to collars, cuffs, waistbands, and necklines. It comes in different weights – light, medium, heavy and it can be iron-on or sewn-in. I usually go for the iron-on variety – which is known as fusible interfacing. Here's how to use it:

- Cut the interfacing. It needs to be the same size as the fabric you're applying it to.

- Heat up the iron, match the temperature to the type of fabric you're about to bond the interfacing to.

- Place the fabric the wrong side up, and lay the sticky side of the interfacing down onto the fabric.

- Put a cloth on top of the interfacing and fabric and press down with the iron until the fabric and interfacing have fused.

- Let everything cool down, and then have a quick check to see if the whole thing has fused nicely. If it hasn't, iron again until it all bonds.

A FEW SIMPLE COMMERCIAL PATTERNS.

You can make lots of things without a pattern, but they are a great basis for getting creative with clothes, without having to embark on a pattern-cutting course. I've got a pattern for a pair of flared trousers, one for Capri pants (the sort that Audrey Hepburn wears in the mad jazz routine in *Funny Face*), a couple of basic skirt patterns, and about 17 versions of a summer sundress pattern that I accidentally buy over and over again. Plus my favourite pattern of all time – for an A-line shift-dress – which is tattered and torn because I've used it so much. It looks pretty uninspiring on the envelope, but I'm always thinking of new ways to make it.

IT COULD BE:

An awayday dress, covered in sewn-on train tickets, just like the one in the London Transport Museum decorated with tram tickets from 1925.

Bedecked in rows of fringes for some Twenties flapper chic. If friends are heading to Spain for their holidays, get them to bring you back a good few metres – it's really cheap there.

Decorated with doilies for some instant lacy elegance.

Used to showcase an expensive tea towel. I know that sounds a little odd, but I spotted a girl in a bar who had pinned a Marimekko forest print tea towel to her dress, and it looked brilliant. She said the towel was too expensive to dry the dishes with, and too nice to store away in a drawer, so she decided to wear it instead.

Covered in embroidery, beads and sequins for a just-out-of-Eden evening dress.

All the patterns I own are easy-to-sew ones, they're straightforward, with no difficult tailoring techniques to master. The back of the pattern will tell you how much fabric you'll need, the length of zip to buy and it'll list any other bits and pieces you might need to finish your outfit, like buttons, hook and eyes, elastic.

Before heading out on a pattern-finding mission, you'll need to have a handle on some key measurements – bust, waist and hips. When you're buying a pattern use *your* measurements, and not your shop dress size – for a top, it's the bust measurement that counts, and head to the hips for skirt or trousers or a dress. If your measurements aren't quite in line with the numbers on the pattern, go for the larger size. Too big and it can be taken in. Too small and you will be the proud owner of yet another lovely cushion cover.

✷ TOP TIP ✷

Look out for pattern special offers. Keep a little notebook of patterns that you like the look of, but don't need urgently: write down the catalogue you saw them in and the pattern number, and when sale time comes around you can stock up for less money.

Here's how to get those numbers (it's best to strip down to your underwear, that way the measurements will be more accurate):

For your bust measurement, loop the tape measure under your arms, across the widest bit of your back and the fullest bit of your bust.

Go for the middle ground next. Tie a piece of ribbon or string loosely around your waist, let it go; where it settles is your natural waistline. Measure around your newly discovered natural waistline.

For your hips, head for where your butt is biggest.

Commercial patterns are often multi-size. You need to know your size so that you can work out which lines to cut around on the pattern. To avoid cutting-out confusion, highlight your size on the pattern tissue paper with a pink fluorescent marker – this makes it much easier to see where your scissors should be going. And if you think you're going to be using your pattern again and again, it might be a good idea to make a copy. Buy some dressmaker's tracing paper from the haberdasher's, and make a replica.

I love buying old-style patterns from charity shops. I can't resist the illustrations on the front – Sixties A-line air hostess dresses, Seventies flared trousers suits, or odd little towelling beach cover-ups like the one that Sean Connery zipped himself into in a Bond film. But, often, when I get them home, half the pattern pieces are missing, so that the dashing dove-coloured car coat, with bell-shaped sleeves is destined never to be made. Also the sizes are wildly different, we've got bigger and taller since the Fifties, so bear in mind your modern-day measurements before embarking on some retro styling.

* TOP TIP *

Once you've cut out your tissue-paper pattern, don't bother trying to refit it back into the envelope. Instead, fold it neatly into a manila envelope, and slip that into a plastic display folder along with the pattern envelope. It'll save you mixing up pattern pieces and you can see at a glance what the pattern is.

And of course, there is FABRIC to think and dream about. I have mountains of it, from charity-shop curtains, to salvaged duvet covers, to a 100cm strip of cherry-red padded silk, printed with elegant white flowers, which I look at often, but can never quite decide to cut. I tend not to buy anything too expensive, attempt to make sure that the fabric's machine washable at a cool temperature, and recycle when I can. Those three rules are pretty much my only requirements; as far as fabric goes, I am prepared to give anything a try. A rain hat made from a bit of a table-cloth, a kimono wrap made from a pale yellow curtain printed with dragons, a dancing skirt created from a satiny duvet cover, a loose dress made from forest green silk, with circles of salmon pink and lemony yellow. Sari shops, market stalls, vintage fairs and haberdashery departments always set my covetous heart beating. I would like to be able to say buy only what you need, but the only thing I can safely say is buy what you like.

And here's a caveat to that proclamation. It's worth having a quantity of dowdy, inexpensive fabric on hand as practice material.

If you've haven't sewed for a while or it's your first time, it's a good idea to have a go on an odd bit of fabric first – a pillowcase that's lost its mate, or a faded duvet cover. That way it doesn't matter one iota if it all goes a little haywire. In fact, I'd always recommend trying something new out on a piece of old cloth. You can run it up quickly, see where it needs a bit of adjustment, and then make the real thing neatly in a piece of pristine printed cotton, or whispery taffeta. It really can prevent heartbreak and ruination.

A lot of the fabric I use in *Lovely Things to Make for Girls of Slender Means* was recycled – reclaimed curtains, T-shirt sleeves, upholstery fabric – rescued from a charity-shop shelf or uncrumpled from the bottom of a cupboard. I wanted to show that it was possible to have a harum-scarum selection of fabric and still make something pretty. So you could make a dress from 100cm of one piece of lovely bright cotton, but you could also make the same dress in 50cm of a rescued duvet cover, and 50cm from fabric bought in a vintage fair – just like the girl I saw the other day who'd, very sweetly, made a dress with a print of small birds on the front and a print of a wood on the back.

When I've used new fabric, I've usually bought it from 150cm bolts of cloth, because I find it's more economical than the smaller 115cm bolts. If you're using narrower, buy more cm. That said, the given measurements in *Lovely Things* are approximate because I am the world's worst measurer – and always have fabric left over. Which hopefully won't be too much of a problem as there are lots of suggestions for using up those scrappy bits of fabric – corsages, bows, patchwork, fabric pom-poms.

A quick note on right sides, wrong sides, widthways, lengthways

The right side of the fabric is the one that's going to be on public view – the outside – and the wrong side is the one that's going to be inside. Usually it's pretty easy to tell which is which – for cord and fake fur, the textured side is the right side; on printed fabric, it's the side where the print is boldest; and if it's a piece of cloth that's completely reversible – a bold cotton, say – you decide which are the right and wrong sides. Chalk a mark onto your designated wrong side, so you won't get confused when it comes to the sewing part.

And when I say fold the fabric widthways, I mean this:

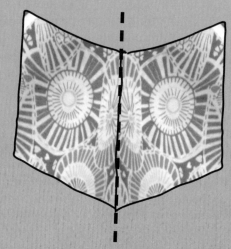

And when I say fold the fabric lengthways, I mean this:

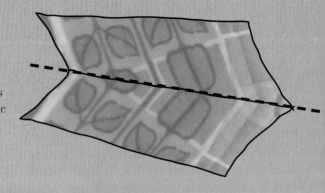

Stitch Craft

I used to be a slapdash girl: cut, sew and go (armed with a pocket full of emergency safety pins for those unravelling moments) was the way I approached dressmaking. Nowadays, I am slightly less haphazard, but still nowhere near the perfection of my friend Helen, whose sewing looks like it was stitched using needles of gold and silken thread delicately harvested from spider's webs.

I've added zigzagging to my repertoire, I sew hems instead of stapling them, I press everything and I have been known to iron interfacing to a garment for a bit of extra structure, but the insides of my frocks (and sometimes the outsides) wouldn't pass muster at a couture sewing inspection. For me, it's never going to be about process and perfection. I'd far rather concentrate on the fun of making something from scratch and then going a bit wild with the sequins when it's all sewn up.

Here's a crash course in the stitches and simple techniques that you'll need to make the lovely things in this book . . .

If they are close enough to see your SEAMS, it's not your seams they're LOOKING at!

19

Sewing by Hand

BACKSTITCH

Backstitch is used at the start and the finish of a line of sewing and stops all your stitching from unravelling, or to repair ripped seams. Make one stitch, and then bring the needle up through the fabric to begin the next stitch. Then put the needle back into the fabric at the end of the last stitch. Bring the needle out again, going forward again but further along, the gap should be the same size as one stitch. Keep inserting the needle in the end of the last stitch and bringing it out one stitch ahead.

RUNNING STITCH

This looks like a series of small, even dashes and is great for gathering fabric.

- ◆ Put a knot in the end of the thread, work the tip of your needle in and out of the fabric a few times, and then pull the needle through.

TACKING

This is a row of longer length running stitch and is handy for holding fabric in position before you sew everything together for good. It stops the fabric from slipping out of place when you're machine sewing and if you tack at each stage of dressmaking, you can see how things are looking and tweak until you're happy. It's easy to undo, snip the knot at the end of the thread and pulllllllll.

Using the Machine

BLANKET STITCH

This is that pretty stitch which graces the edges of old-fashioned woollen blankets, but you can use it to prettify the hem of a poncho, or the cuff of a cardigan or the snipped edges of a piecemeal jumper.

◆ Anchor the thread to the wrong side of your fabric with a little backstitch.

◆ Insert the needle through the fabric a little way down from the top edge. Don't pull the thread all the way through.

◆ Leave a loop of thread at the edge of the fabric.

◆ Slip the needle and thread through the loop.

◆ Repeat.

STRAIGHT STITCH

This is the one you'll use the most. As it sounds, it's a line of, er, straight stitches and is used on seams, hems, just about everything.

◆ Set the stitch selector to straight, slowly sew a few stitches, then flip the reverse lever and go back over your stitches (this is known as backstitching and will keep your sewing secure).

◆ Now go forward again, slowly and steadily, until you reach the end.

◆ Backstitch again for a few stitches. Cut the thread. You have now successfully sewn a row of straight stitches.

ZIGZAG STITCH

This stitch looks like perfect thready peaks and is used to stop the raw edges of fabric from fraying.

◆ Change the stitch selector to the zigzag options.

◆ Sew close to the edge of the fabric. Hey presto, disintegration halted.

STAY-STITCHING

I'd often read this instruction on a pattern and went ahead and ignored it. But then I tried it, and suddenly sewing necks and armholes became so much easier. Fabric can stretch out of shape when you cut it, a line of stay-stitching will stop that awryness happening. All you have to do is sew a line of straight stitches, about ½ cm in from the edge. When stay-stitching a neckline, start at the outer edge and sew towards the middle. Stop. Head over to the other side, start at the outer edge and sew back to the middle again.

SEAMS

There are many kinds of seams out there, but the straight seam is the one you'll use the most. All this involves is sewing the right sides of the fabric together a little bit from the edges. That little distance is known as the seam allowance. Most commercial patterns have a seam allowance of 1.5cm, but I usually go for 1cm.

◆ Zigzag the edges of the fabric.

◆ Pin the fabric, right sides together. Start with a few backstitches (all you have to do is hold the reverse knob for a couple of seconds) and then sew 1cm in from the edge. Flip a few more backstitches when you reach the end to make sure nothing comes undone.

◆ Press.

NOTCHES, CLIPS, AND A SPOT OF LAYERING

Some seams are bulky; to make them lie nice and flat, a bit of scissor work is needed.

On a seam that curves inward, clip. With the tip of your scissors, snip into the seam allowance, like this, but be very carefully not to cut toooooo far and undo all stitches. Press the seams open when you've finished snipping

On a seam that curves outwards, notch – which means cutting out 'V'-shaped wedges. Press the seam open.

Layering is also known as grading, and is all about getting rid of excess fabric in a seam. To trim a seam, cut both seam allowances together to about half their original width, and then go ahead and press. Grading means that you cut the seam allowances to different widths. The seam allowance that nestles against your body should be wider, the one that's not next to skin, thinner.

DARTS

Darts are used to give shape to the fabric where it settles at the curvy bits of the body – mainly on the bust, waist and hips. A dart is a tapering seam, stitched to a point, in a nice triangular shape.

◆ On the wrong side of the fabric, mark

where the dart should go with tailor's chalk (see below for the info on marking).

◆ Fold the marked-out dart in half, with the right sides of the fabric together.

◆ You could pin or tack the dart in place, but I usually head straight for the sewing machine.

◆ Start sewing at the fullest bit, and head in a straight line to the point. Go slowly to avoid puckers and scrunches.

◆ For a bust dart, backstitch is not the way to go. Instead, leave long tails of thread at the beginning of the dart and at the end, and tie little knots, that way the dart will lie beautifully flat.

◆ Press. In general bust darts are pressed downwards, darts at the waist of a skirt are pressed towards the middle of your fine garment.

On Your Marks

Sometimes you want to remind yourself where exactly a bust dart should go, or the exact location of the zip. You can guess (and I often do with interesting results), but for accuracy it really is best to follow the pattern guidelines. You'll need pins and tailor's chalk.

◆ Flip the fabric so that the wrong side is up.

◆ Push pins through the dots on the pattern into the fabric.

◆ Lift the pattern paper, but don't take the pins out of the fabric.

◆ With the tailor's chalk, clearly mark where the pins are sticking in the fabric.

◆ Do the same with the underside. Take out the pins. Marked? Set? Gooooooo.

Hems

This is the one I use most; for other suggestions, head to Spring, and the 'How To Repair A Hem' section on page 54.

◆ Try on the garment first to decide how long or short you want it.

◆ Zigzag the edge of the fabric.

◆ Press a skinny hem to the wrong side of the fabric.

◆ Press a deeper hem to the wrong side of the fabric; the skinny hem will be hidden under the deeper hem.

◆ Then sew, with a straight stitch, as close to the hem's edge, as possible.

◆ Press again.

ZIPS

I always used to avoid making anything with a zip in it, but then I realised they're actually simple to do. You're going to need a zipper foot for the best results, but all new machines have them.

◆ Sew the seam, but leave enough room for the zip.

◆ You can tack the rest of the seam closed by hand. Or set your machine to the longest stitch length and tack it that way.

◆ Press the seam open.

◆ Place the closed zipper face down onto the seam on the wrong side of the fabric. Make sure it's nice and straight, and that it's lined up with the centre of your seam.

◆ Tack the zip to the seam allowance by hand, or with your machine.

◆ Turn the fabric over, and put the zipper foot onto the machine. Sew the zip in place, remembering to backstitch at the start and at the finishing line.

◆ Stitch across the bottom of the zip to make it secure.

◆ Rip out all your tacking with a seam ripper. (Although sometimes I leave it in as evidence.)

A quick reminder of what to do before you get down to the sewing bit

Wash the fabric first. Another instruction I have ignored, only to find myself holding my breath to do up the zip after a carefully made dress has diminished after I put it in the machine. A lot of fabric is pre-shrunk, but to avoid any 'it's too tiiiight' surprises, it's worth popping it in the washing machine before you transform that lovely piece of printed cotton into something nicely slinky.

Iron the fabric. Wrinkly fabric will result in an askew garment, and once you cut there's NO turning back.

Read all the instructions. A bit dull, I know, but it's good to know what order things come in, and what to expect, just in case you have to brush up on a technique, or hurry to the shops to buy a forgotten zip.

If you're using a commercial pattern, assemble the pattern pieces you need, and then put away the ones that you don't need for the minute, that way you won't have to fight your way through tearable clouds of temporarily abandoned tissue paper to find the ringing phone.

Double check for wrinkles and crinkles on the fabric; if you find any lurking, vanish them with the iron. I know I've said this twice, but I have a very bad habit of walking over the my freshly ironed fabric to make a cup of tea, without realising quite how badly I've scrunched it up again. Result? Some unintentionally askew skirts.

Pin the pattern pieces to the fabric. Make sure everything's smooth, and if you're using a commercial pattern, pin the pattern pieces exactly the way it's shown in the layout diagram – that way everything will hang beautifully.

Take your time for the next bit, there's less likely to be mistakes and mishaps if you proceed at a sedate pace. Maybe have a look at the treetops out of the window, or put on a record, before getting busy with the scissors. Bad stitches can be undone, the cutting part is forever.

Cut very carefully.

Transfer the pattern marks, like where the bust darts should go, or where the zip will reside, onto the wrong side of your fabric.

Cut out the interfacing, if you need it. Have a quick lie down on the floor to recuperate. And then…

HEY HO...
let's
SEW!

The birds are singing, and the day is bright...
Nature is casting off the gloomy sleepiness of winter, SPRING clothes should too.

The birds are singing and the days are bright, and every tree has a little green bud, the hint of unfurling gold leaf. Nature is casting off the gloom and sleepiness of winter, and spring clothes should too. Flannel vests should be consigned to bottom drawers, and big woolly jumpers carefully repaired and stored away with lavender bags, so that they'll smell of summer meadows when the dark days of winter come calling again. Spring is the perfect time for a spot of re-appraisal, and adventurousness, so mend things, restore buttons, repair hems, and transform cardigans with a strip of velvet ribbon and a cascade of pearly buttons. And then set about making new things from the stuff that's already nestling in your wardrobe – turn a pretty patterned duvet cover into a pair of retro knickers, or create a rain hat from a spare piece of plastic tablecloth fabric.

I always dream of running away to sea at this time of year, thinking that I will have a whole new life that involves practical duffel bags and impractical origami earrings. But I am more likely to be found at home ransacking the kitchen cupboards for out-of-date dry goods in an endeavour to make little embroidered brooches stuffed with yellow split peas, or tipping out a big handful of sequins and making a scarf that is to remind me of the shimmery sea on a sunlit morning, when I am still, somehow a land lubber.

But it really is all about things coming into bloom. I spend a lot of the time thinking of clothes you can grow. Artist Suzanne Lee is busy at the moment optimistically growing fabric in large trays, brimming with green tea and sugared water. The solution transforms itself into sheets of cellulose, which might, with circular elegance, end up as dresses to drink tea in. (She's also discovered that Japanese fire-fighters' outfits were made from paper in ancient times, and coated with the juice of unripe persimmons to make them flame resistant.)

Surely it couldn't be that hard to magic up cress dresses, with mustard seed cuffs and collars, lichen handkerchiefs, moss scarves? But what I'd really love is a sweet pea frock. Seeds, compost and sunshine might not be the ideal components of a dressmaking endeavour, but a handful of fake flowers, some beads and a needle and thread can transform a plain dress into something blooming. I bought loads of flowers from the pound shop – on the shelf they did look a bit shabby, but pruned from their plastic stems, and with their cheap leaves snipped away, they ended up looking very chic.

FLOWER HEADBANDS

The nomadic Surma and Mursi tribes, who live in the Oma valley, Ethiopia, use the flora and fauna that surround them to fashion the most beautiful accessories, from ephemeral head dresses garlanded with flowers to hats woven from feathered grasses and decorated with delicate mushrooms, snail shells and brightly coloured fruits. Photographer Hans Silvester says, 'They can take any material from the plant world – leaf, stem, flower, grass, root – and instantly transform it into an accessory that has come straight from a fantasy or fairytale, without the slightest tinge of absurdity.' Smitten by his images and their creations I've used artificial flowers and stretchy headbands to bloom without bombast.

You'll need:
A *pack of* STRETCHY HEADBANDS
A *selection of pound-shop* FAKE FLOWERS *or*
    some FAKE ROSE PETALS
NEEDLE
THREAD

Gently remove all the plastic bits that hold the pound-shop flowers together.

Re-fashion the separated petals into flowers, as small, medium or extra large, by hand-sewing layers of petals together.

Hand-sew the flower onto the stretchy headband.

If you are going to cover the headband completely with floral exuberance, sew each blossom on separately, and remember that the headband will streeeeetch when it goes around your head so, if you don't want gaps, sew the blooms very closely together.

They also look lovely as a necklace – just pull the headband over your head, and let it nestle against your collarbone.

In *The Picture of Dorian Gray*, Oscar Wilde's modern butterfly, the Duchess of Monmouth, also has good advice to follow on the hat front, inspired by the resourcefulness of her maid. 'Why, she invents hats for me. You remember the one I wore at Lady Hilstone's garden party? Well, she made it out of nothing. All good hats are made out of nothing.'

31

A Hat Made Out of Practically Nothing

YOU'LL NEED:

A STIFF HAIRBAND *or* A SMALL HAT FOUNDATION *(found in a millinery supply shop)*
GROS-GRAIN RIBBON
POUND-SHOP FLOWERS
LITTLE CIRCLES *of* FELT *or* A FEW FLOWER PETALS
MILLINER'S NET
GLUE
NEEDLE & THREAD

Wind the ribbon around the hairband, gluing in place as you go.

Gently take apart the pound-shop flowers. Discard the plastic bits.

Re-construct the flowers by sewing them together.

Glue the blooms to the hairband or hat foundation.

On the underside of the headband, glue a petal to the back of the flower, to keep your bloom more firmly in place.

Wait until the glue is REALLY DRY, and then try on the hairband. Wet glue and dry hair is a very sticky combination. Measure enough of the milliner's net to cover your eyes mysteriously, and add an extra centimetre or two for sewing room.

Sew the net, with tiny neat stitches, to the ribbon.

Apply some dark eyeliner. Smoulder.

Once you've seen how easy it is to make flowers, why stop there? You can make hearts and plump kissable lips from felt and stuff them with fabric scraps. Or perch soot-coloured birds and ash-smudged leaves on a dark hairband for a midnight-forest look.

A RAIN-DRENCHED GARDEN DRESS

I made this dress with some of the seams outside and the fabric edges left raggedy to make it look even more storm-damaged and weather-worn.

YOU'LL NEED:

A READY-MADE DRESS *in a plain colour, with a* **FITTED TOP** *and a* **FULLER SKIRT** *(the one on page 110 should do the trick)*

FAKE FLOWERS *(I used a selection from the pound-shop and some fake rose petals – Ikea sell them for about £2 a box)*

A SMALL HANDFUL *of* **BEADS**

NEEDLE

THREAD

Gently remove all the plastic bits that hold the pound-shop flowers together.

Re-fashion the separated petals into small, medium or extra-large flowers by hand-sewing layers of petals together. Do the same if you're using fake rose petals.

Hand-sew silvery beads onto some of the petals.

Hand-sew a small garland of them down one shoulder of the dress.

Grab a handful of petals and sprinkle them over the skirt of the dress. Hand-sew them where they've landed.

Hand-sew on some silvery beads as raindrops for a dress that looks like an early-flowering rose undone by a spring storm.

33

A RAIN HAT

To save your hair from spring downpours, make a little rain hat from a piece of thin, plastic tablecloth material. You could use oilcloth, but it might be a bit tough to sew and a bit uncomfortable to wear.

YOU'LL NEED:
1 PIECE *of* WATERPROOF FABRIC,
   80CM X 60CM
PINS
NEWSPAPER
PEN
NEEDLE & THREAD
15CM DIAMETER BOWL, *or* COMPASS
PAPER SCISSORS
TAILOR'S CHALK

Make a rough paper pattern for your rainy day hat. Place your bowl on 16cm sq of newspaper. Draw round it – this is the crown of your beau chapeau. Then cut out a side panel, and a piece for the brim (see pictures).

On the wrong side of the fabric, draw around the paper circle with the tailor's chalk.

Fold the fabric in half, lengthways, right sides together, and put the side panel and the brim on the fold (see picture) and cut them out. Cut out another brim piece on the fold.

With the right sides together, sew the side seam of the side band.

With the right sides together, pin the side band to the crown and sew.

CROWN
x1

SIDE PANEL
x1

BRIM x1

With the right sides together, pin the brim pieces, and sew all the way around. Notch the seam, taking care not to snip into your stitches.

Turn the brim the right way out.

Tack around the inner edge, near the edge to keep the brim pieces aligned. Then pin the side band to the brim, right sides together.

Sew, turn the hat the right way round and await a spring rain shower.

35

A hoist on your shoulder, runaway to sea duffel bag

I love films where the heroine runs away to sea after a high-falutin' officer, who proves unworthy of her affections. She eventually falls for the lovely midshipman, who has a heart tattoo, a penchant for sea shanties, drinking tots of rum and dancing the hornpipe on the deck of a pitching ship. If I really was that girl, I'd wait until there was enough blue in the sky to run up a pair of wide-legged sailor trousers and then I'd head for the port. I'd pack my get-away wardrobe in a duffel bag, and my worldly goods would include many pairs of shore-leave knickers. I'd also pack a few little treats – a tulle wrap, a sequinned neck scarf, and a corsage. Because the voyage would be long, I'd also pack a book on origami, and spend my stowaway hours making origami earrings, either made from old maps, perfect for girls who like to travel but have a shaky sense of direction, or constructed from brightly coloured note paper, with secret messages hidden in the folds.

YOU'LL NEED:

1 PIECE *of* STURDY FABRIC, 95CM X 65CM
1 EXTRA SQUARE *of* STURDY FABRIC,
    30CM X 30CM
1 PIECE *of* PRETTY LINING FABRIC,
    85CM X 60CM
1 EXTRA SQUARE *of* PRETTY LINING FABRIC,
    30CM X 30CM
1 SQUARE *of* MEDIUM FUSIBLE INTERFACING,
    30CM X 30CM
2.5M JUMBO CORD
1 METAL CURTAIN RING *or* A D-RING
10CM STRONG COTTON TAPE
6 CLIP-TOGETHER CURTAIN RINGS
AN UN-METRIC 12-INCH SINGLE *(or a compass*
    if you've swapped everything on to your mp3
    player)
TAILOR'S CHALK
IRON

Iron the fusible interfacing to the wrong side of the 30cm x 30cm square of sturdy fabric.

Draw around your favourite 12-inch with the tailor's chalk on the interfaced fabric. (If you, alas, alack, lack a record collection, use a compass, the diameter is about 25cm.)

Cut around the circle. This is the base of the duffel bag. Zigzag the edges.

Zigzag the edges of the 95cm x 65cm piece of sturdy fabric.

Thread the 10cm of cotton tape through the D-ring. Pin the ends to the wrong side of the piece of sturdy fabric, about 2cm from the bottom edge.

With the right sides together, pin the sturdy fabric into a tube. The cotton tape is sewn into the side seam, with the tape ends inside the bag, and the loop and D-ring outside the bag. This is where you are going to thread the jumbo cord a little later.

Sew the pinned seam.

Whip out the pins on the side seam, and with the right sides together, pin the lower edge of the bag to the interfaced circle of fabric.

Notch the seam to neaten it.

Turn down a hem of 5cm on the top edge of the bag, and sew.

Now for the lining. Using the 12-inch paper pattern, cut out a circle from the 30cm x 30cm lining fabric.

Fold it in half, lengthways, with the right sides together, pin the side seam and sew it into a tube.

With the right sides together, pin the tube to the lining circle. Sew. Turn a 5cm hem under and press. Pop the lining inside the bag and pin it just under the turned-down hem of the sturdy fabric. Sew it as neatly as you can, as your stitches will be seen on the outside.

To make the holes for the jumbo cord, draw around the inside of the plastic rings, which you evenly place around the top of the sturdy fabric, just below the top edge. Carefully cut the circles out, by folding the hem over, and cutting around the marked semi-circles. Then neatly clip and lock the two sides of your plastic curtain rings to the front and back of the cut-out circles.

Weave the rope in and out of the holes, so that the two ends of the rope come out either side of the back seam. Pull the rope ends through the metal curtain ring at the bottom of the bag and tie a giant knot to keep it nice and shipshape and secure.

Check the tides, practise drinking tots of rum, be ready to abscond.

ORIGAMI EARRINGS

These earrings are delicately ephemeral. Make them to match your outfit, and when they crumple re-use the earring fittings and the jump rings to make new ones.

YOU'LL NEED:

ORIGAMI PAPER, *or* TISSUE PAPER, *or* OLD, WEATHER-BEATEN MAPS

EARRING FITTINGS

JUMP RINGS (*these are little metal circles that connect bits of jewellery together*)

PLIERS

A BOOK ON ORIGAMI

GLUE

NEEDLE & THREAD

Peruse your origami book for something that's not too difficult and not too big.

Fold your paper into your chosen design.

Carefully glue a jump ring to the top of your paper creation. Or you can hand-sew the jump rings to the paper with a small needle and fine thread.

Open the little loop on the earring fitting with the pliers.

Pop the jump ring onto the loop.

Close the little loop with the pliers.

39

A FABRIC Corsage

A corsage is a lovely addition to the lapel of a jacket, the flap of a bag, the waist of a belt.

YOU'LL NEED:
1 STRIP of FABRIC 35CM X 25CM
or 70CM X 13CM
SEQUINS
1 BUTTON
1 SAFETY PIN or BROOCH BACK
A COMPASS or THE LID OF THE SUGAR BOWL
TAILOR'S CHALK
PINKING SHEARS
SCISSORS
NEEDLE & THREAD
SPRAY STARCH (optional)

Using a school compass or the lid of the sugar bowl, draw six circles onto the wrong side of the fabric with the tailor's chalk.

Cut out the circles with the pinking shears.

Trim about 1.5cm from the edges of three of the circles, so that they're smaller than the other three.

With the scissors, cut three slits at regular intervals on all six circles, stopping about 1.5cm from the centre of each circle.

Taking each circle in turn, sew the edges of each slit together, so that the flat circles become curved into a little cup.

Hand-sew on some sequins.

Sew the button into the middle of one of the smaller circles.

Now sew all the cup-shaped circles together, making sure that the littlest circles go on the top, and the bigger ones are on the bottom.

Sew a safety pin or brooch back to the back of the corsage.

Fluff out the petals.

To make your corsage more perky, mist with spray starch and leave to dry.

A DANGLY SEQUINED SCARF

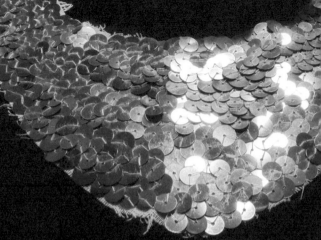

There's something very dashing about a little neck scarf, especially if it shimmers and shines with rows of overlapping sequins, like the pale blues and greens of the waves on the ocean, with a glimmer of gold to suggest the sparkle of spring sunshine. I used not very large sequins here, and it took ages to sew. For a faster scarf, use huge sequins, but make sure they overlap a little for maximum fabric coverage.

YOU'LL NEED:

1 SQUARE OF FABRIC, 60CM X 60CM.
   I used very soft cotton, because it drapes so nicely. Silk would be lovely too, or tulle.
SEQUINS. *I used blue and green 8mm paillettes and gold 10mm ones.*
NEEDLE & THREAD

Cut the fabric in half.

Then cut the 2 pieces into this sort of shape:

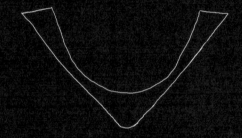

I keep the back nice and curvy, but you could make it straight, like a sailor's collar.

Sew the sequins onto one of the pieces of fabric, leave a tiny sequin-free gap around the edges of the fabric.

Hand-sew the other piece of fabric to the underside of the sequinned side, to hide your thready bits, with tiny neat stitches, if you like, but there's something gallant about leaving your handiwork on display.

A
Small but Jaunty
SEQUINED SCARF

YOU'LL NEED:
40CM *of* VERY WIDE VELVET RIBBON
LARGE SEQUINS
1M *of* THINNER VELVET RIBBON
NEEDLE & THREAD

Sew the sequins onto the wide velvet ribbon, so that the sequins overlap.

Sew the thinner velvet ribbon to each end of the wide be-sequinned velvet. Drape the scarf around your neck, and tie a velvet bow with the trailing ends of the ribbon.

And if you use more velvet ribbon and sequins this is lovely as a belt too.

Gay Abandon KNICKERS

GUEST STAR Amy Newman makes Gay Abandon Knickers from vintage fabric and old tees, from lovely salvaged duvets and pillowcases washed to softness, and crisp new cotton printed with retro designs.

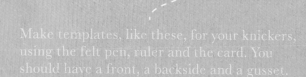

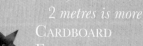

YOU'LL NEED:

50CM *of* COTTON *for a small pair of knickers*
1 *piece of* COTTON FABRIC *for the gusset –*
   an old tee would be perfect
Thin, decorative KNICKER ELASTIC,
   2 metres is more than enough

CARDBOARD
FELT PEN
RULER
SCISSORS
TAILOR'S CHALK
IRON
LIGHTER *or* A MATCH
NEEDLE & THREAD

Make templates, like these, for your knickers, using the felt pen, ruler and the card. You should have a front, a backside and a gusset.

Place the templates on the wrong side of the fabric of your choice.

Using the tailor's chalk draw around the templates on the fabric. Or pin the templates.

Cut the fabric out.

With the right sides of the fabric together, sew the front to the back at the gusset.

Press the little gusset seam open.

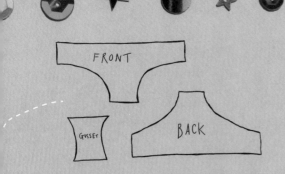

FRONT

GUSSET

BACK

Place the gusset panel right side down on the inside of the knickers with the back (wider) end towards the top of the front piece of knickers. Stitch the narrower end of the gusset panel to the knickers front.

Flip the gusset panel over so that it's in the right place. Press.

Press a narrow hem on the wider end of the panel at the back.

Stitch this in place, close to the edge of the fold.

With the wrong sides together, stitch the side seams, with a very narrow seam.

Then turn the knickers inside out, and sew another narrow seam on each of the sides… et voilà, you have stitched a French seam, and very tidy it is too.

Sew a small hem along the waist of the knickers.

And then sew small hems around the knicker legs.

Now for the elastic, and a change of stitch. Turn the stitch-selector dial on your machine to the broken zigzag stitch.

Singe the end of the elastic to stop it from fraying. A quick waft through the flame is all you need – any more and you'll have a pile of molten fabric on your hands. Literally.

The tricky bit is coming up now. Pull the elastic taut as you sew it to the inside of your knicker fabric. When you let go, everything should ruffle up nicely. Sew the elastic to the wrong side of the knickers, so that the pretty decorative edge peeps over the fabric, and the main bit of the elastic is lined up with the top of the seams. Start with the waist.

Then do the same around the knicker legs – continue pulling the elastic tautly, but *not in the gusset area* . . . as that would be most uncomfortable, madam. Instead sew the elastic on gently here, before returning to the taut stance for the rest of the knickers.

Snip stray threads and you're good to go-go in your shore-leave knickers.

(Don't forget to change the top or bottom thread colours if you are using contrasting trim or gusset.)

SPRING SEEMS THE PERFECT TIME TO EMBARK ON A SEASON OF SALVAGE. WANDER AROUND YOUR HOUSE + REAPPRAISE YOUR POSSESSIONS WITH AN EYE TO TRANSFORMING THEM INTO SOMETHING ELSE, REPAIRING OR MAKING NEW ACCESSORIES FROM SOME OLD THINGS. BUT MAKE AN APRON BEFORE YOU START, IT'S ALWAYS NICE TO BE APPROPRIATELY ATTIRED.

A Cute Apron

Aprons are easy to make – in nostalgic gingham, traffic-light-bright cotton or delicate shades of cup-cake-coloured chintz, or left-over big-onions furnishing fabric. Or you could unpick a couple of old, patterned pillowcases for a touch of Fifties domesticity. Add pockets with ric-rac edging, stencilled apples, fabric-painted flowers.

YOU'LL NEED:
A RECTANGLE *of* CHEERY CHERRY *(the colour is up to you)* THICKISH COTTON 68CM X 50CM
1 LONG, THIN PIECE *of* FABRIC 200CM X 6CM, *or* 2 LONG THIN BITS *of* FABRIC, 100CM X 6CM *(for the waistband and ties)*
IRON
PINS
A FEATHER DUSTER *(optional)*
HAIR COMB *(optional)*
GLUE *(optional)*

Press a skinny little hem on the long ties onto the wrong side of the fabric.

Press a skinny little hem on the narrow ends of the ties.

Press a skinny hem around the three sides of the apron rectangle: on both 50cm sides and on one of the 68cm edges, again onto the wrong side of the fabric.

Now turn those hems over again, so that the zigzag edge is nicely hidden. Press. And then sew.

Press the long apron ties in half, lengthways, wrong sides together.

Position the ties along the top edge of the apron, like a fabric sandwich . . . , the filing is the apron edge.

Pin in place.

Put your foot to the pedal of the sewing machine and whiz a lovely line of top stitches along the lower edge of the first apron tie and then across the apron and then along the lower edge of the second tie.

Sew across the narrow ends of the ties.

Tie around your waist, and watch a Doris Day movie whilst making a list of your tasks for the day. Make a hair ornament from the feather duster, the glue and the hair comb.

Zigzag the edges of the apron rectangle to stop all the fabric fraying.

Zigzag the edges of the long rectangles.

If you are using two long, thin pieces for the waist tie: with the right sides together, sew the two pieces together along one of those 6cm edges.

Press the seam open and flat.

A PING-PONG BALL
necklace

I've always coveted oversize necklaces, with oversized prices, in fashion magazines, so I set about thinking of how to recreate one at home. I was lucky enough to find 24 ping-pong balls, possibly left over from the table-tennis tournaments I played with my brother and sister in the kitchen. We didn't have bats – we used a big cheese board and a very small spatula made in school woodwork – or a net, but we had a lot of arguments. I used slate-grey, left-over curtain fabric to make big beads, but with the addition of a plush velvet ribbon and ghost-pale fabric with a delicate sheen, the ping-pong balls are transformed into giant pearls.

YOU'LL NEED:
2 *strips of* FABRIC, 13CM X 150CM
24 PING-PONG BALLS *(If you don't have a well-stocked games cupboard, you can buy them in packs of 12 from the pound shop)*
VELVET *or* SATIN RIBBON
THIN SATIN RIBBON *in* DIFFERENT COLOURS
NEEDLE & THREAD

Fold the first strip of fabric in half, lengthways, right sides together. Machine-sew along one short edge and then along the long edge of the fabric to create a long, long, long tube.

Turn the tube the right way out.

Pop a ping-pong ball into the tube, but halt its progress before it reaches the end. Put a twist in the end of the tube, and hand-sew the twist in place.

Then twist the section of tube that comes after the ping-pong ball. Hand-sew that twist in place. Then pop the next ping-pong into the tube, twist the fabric tube, and hand-sew that twist.

Do that with 12 of the ping-pong balls. Turn the ends of the tube in and hand-sew a line of stitches to neaten up the tube, and add a final twist.

Repeat with the other strip of fabric and a dozen ping-pong balls.

Sew the 2 giant pearl strands to the velvet ribbon or satin ribbon.

Tie small satin ribbons in between the ping-pong pearls.

YELLOW SPLIT-PEA BADGES

The kitchen cupboard, and some very out-of-date yellow split peas, can also be a source for some askew jewellery. I found a packet at the back that had been nestling there since 2006. Once when my brother opened a packet of past-its-sell-by-date porridge oats, a confetti of moths fluttered out. There were no moths this time, and the pulses were a perfect filling for little embroidered badges.

YOU'LL NEED:

A HANDFUL *of* YELLOW SPLIT PEAS *(they don't have to be out-of-date ones, you could use ones that were still cookable, that way your jewellery is dual purpose, in straitened times you could boil it up for soup)*

2 RECTANGLES *of* COTTON *or* CALICO APPROX 9CM X 12CM

SPARKLY THREAD

UNSPARKLY THREAD

SCRAPS *of* PATTERNED FABRIC

BUTTON(S)

SAFETY PIN *or a* BROOCH BACK

A PERMANENT MARKER *or a* FABRIC PEN

A PIZZA LEAFLET

NEEDLE & THREAD

Draw a motif onto one piece of the cotton or calico with the permanent marker or fabric pen. I had to draw vague self-portraits because I can't draw much else.

Embroider features, add sparkly thread to the hair and backstitch blushes to the cheeks.

Cut snippets of patterned fabric into the shapes of mini tees and shirts. Sew on a couple of buttons.

Grab the second bit of cotton/calico, and with the right sides together, sew the two pieces together, either as a rectangle, or in the shape of your drawing. Don't sew too close to the edge of your outline though, leave a little room. And don't sew all the way around, leave a gap.

Turn the shape the right way out.

Make a little chute out of the pizza leaflet. Use this to funnel the yellow split peas into the brooch

Sew up the gap.

Attach the safety pin, or sew on the brooch back.

Your brooch doesn't have to be a self-portrait, you can cut out flowers from old duvet covers or curtains, bird shapes from pillowcases, or red felt hearts for a Valentine's Day decoration. And you could replace the split peas with the pulse of your choice – as long as they're dried – the tinned variety might be a bit messy.

How to Sew on a Button

I know how to sew on a button, but sometimes I don't actually do it. My favourite (shop bought) coat has safety pins on the sleeves and is held together with button badges instead of buttons. This was initially an on-the-spot repair – one of the buttons disappeared on a chilly day, so I pinned on a Betty and the Werewolves badge to stop the winds intruding in the gap in my coat. But it looked so nice, that I decided it might not be a bad plan to swap all coat buttons for badges in the future.

In case you're not willing to forgo buttons just yet, here's a quick reminder of how to button up.

To make sure that you sew your wobbly button on in the right place, overlap the edge of your garment as if you were going to do it up.

Then stick a pin through the buttonhole, near the edge of your garment, the centre of the button should be sewn here.

Thread up your needle with a nice length of thread, and in a colour that matches your garment.

Anchor your thread with a couple of tiny backstitches on the wrong side of the garment.

If it's a two-hole flat button, stitch up through one hole in the button and down through the other. Repeat this step about 6 times.

Finish off with a couple of back stitches so that the sewing is nice and secure.

If it's a four-hole button, you can sew in parallel across the two top holes, and then across the 2 bottom holes

Or in cross shape.

Or in a square.

Keep sewing until the button is safely sewn in place. A couple of backstitches will make sure the button doesn't pop off again.

How To Repair a Hem

I am forever catching my hems in the heels of my shoes. Luckily there are a variety of ways to ensure a tumbled-down hem can be rebuilt.

The office stationary cupboard can always supply essential items for a raggedy hem repair. STAPLE the hem back in place, making sure that the sharp bits of the staple are on the inside, and then stick a strip of masking tape over the back of the staples to avoid nasty snags or scrapes.

You could bypass the staples altogether and go straight to the TAPE option, but a metal glint along the hem of a skirt is quite a nice finishing feature.

Use WUNDAWEB – this is iron-on tape that secures a hem in seconds. Fold the hem, insert the Wundaweb in the fold, press with a hot iron, et voilà, hem finished, no sewing.

A squirt of FABRIC GLUE can do the job too.

The HAND-STITCHED repair will take longer, but will be more secure.

FOLD up the unravelled bit of hem so that it matches with the bit that hasn't come undone. Press it into place with an IRON.

Thread up your needle, and do a little BACKSTITCH so that your sewing won't come undone.

With the point of your needle, pick up a couple of threads of the fabric right next to the folded edge of the hem. Push the needle diagonally through the fold of the hem, and pull through.

Move a little to the left, pick up another couple of threads of the fabric and repeat all of the above steps, all the way along the repair site, in nice, evenly spaced stitches.

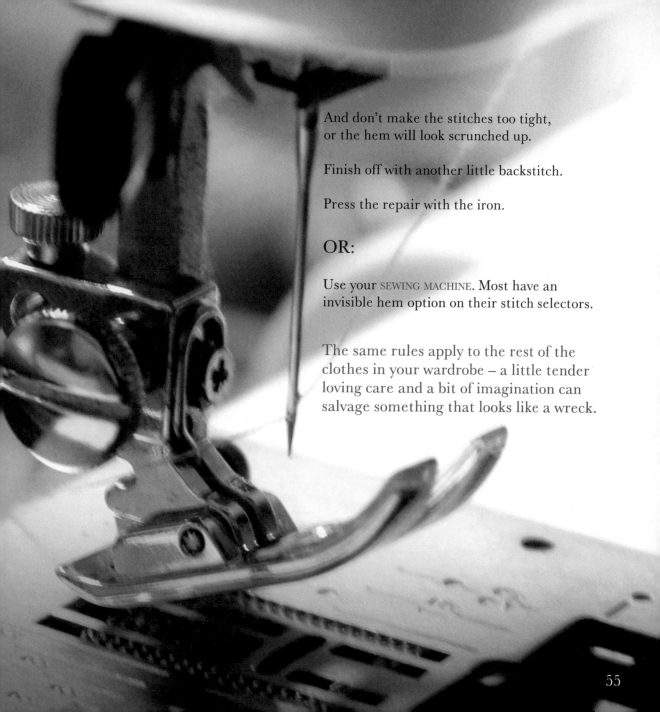

And don't make the stitches too tight,
or the hem will look scrunched up.

Finish off with another little backstitch.

Press the repair with the iron.

OR:

Use your SEWING MACHINE. Most have an
invisible hem option on their stitch selectors.

The same rules apply to the rest of the
clothes in your wardrobe – a little tender
loving care and a bit of imagination can
salvage something that looks like a wreck.

SEVEN THINGS to do with your FAVOURITE TEE

Add a cascade of buttons. All you need is needle and thread, a handful of buttons and a spare half an hour. You could sew the buttons around the neck of the tee in a nice orderly pattern, or sew them higgledy-piggledy over the sleeves, in the shape of epaulettes for a bit of military chic, or in a wild rumpus from one of the shoulders.

With a big, baggy tee snip off the sleeves, cut away a big swathe of fabric from the bottom, and take it in at the sides. Save the sleeves – you can use them as a lining for the sunglasses case (see page 80) or as part of the reversible mittens (see page 200). Trim away the ribbed binding at the neck and use the cut swathe of fabric from the bottom to make a cowl neck. With the right sides together, sew the cut-away fabric into a tube, then sew that tube to the neck of the tee, sew on some big paillette sequins for a disco-dolly look.

Long-sleeved stripy tees can be transformed into short-sleeved stripy tees with the look of an optical illusion. Cut the sleeves; roll a little hem under to stop them from fraying. Cut open the snipped-off bit of the sleeves, cut circles out of the fabric and zigzag the edges of the circles to stop them fraying. Sew the circles to your tee with the stripes on the circles going a different way from the stripes on the tee.

Or fold the tee in half. Cut off the sleeves diagonally, beginning at the underarm, and stopping at the collar edge. Unfold the tee and smooth out the fabric. Cut off the ribbed edge, and then fold the neck over, front and back, to make a channel along each of the top edges. Sew the channels in place. Find 200cm of pretty wide ribbon, cut it in half, and thread it through the channels, one ribbon at the front, one at the back. Tie the ribbons in big bows on each shoulder.

Paper doilies and spray paint will gave a faded tee a lovely, lacy look. Head outside. Slide a sheet of newspaper or cardboard in between the front and back of the tee. Place the doilies on the tee. Aim the nozzle of the can about 30cm from the fabric and press. I used shocking pink, pale blue and metallic gold, and the end result looks a bit ike a Monet daydream. Spray paint isn't the only way to add a bit of colour… fabric pens and paints are good for designing pretty pictures, angry slogans, askew polka dots. Or you could dye the whole tee with a packet of Dylon, a washing machine and 1lb of salt. The salt's there to open the pores in the fabric so that the colour really takes. And instead of dallying with doilies, you can whip up a stencil with a sharp craft knife, a steady hand and a piece of thin card.

A bit of appliqué can look just fine too. Cut big flowers (or whatever shape you fancy) from some cotton fabric. If the fabric is floppy, you could iron on some interfacing to the back of the blooms and then zigzag around the flowers' edges to stop them fraying; and then sew them to your tee.

I like a tarnished-looking tee. To add a little wear and tear, sandpaper moth holes in the fabric. Or carefully cut out almond-shaped holes in the body of the tee – it looks surprisingly pretty. You could also slash the front of the tee, like the rungs on a ladder, and sew a panel of fabric behind the rungs as a cheeky homage to Henry VIII's slashed doublet and hose.

James Dean managed to look coolly dishevelled in a raggle-taggle jumper, just look on the internet at the famous 'Torn Sweater' photos, I don't have the required nonchalance to carry off Jimmy D's holey look and instead appear on the borderline of unkempt. Handily, it is easy to revitalise scruffy old pullovers. The easiest thing to do is to turn them inside out. I have a lovely fine knit charcoal grey jumper that went bobbly. Tempted, but too afraid to actually buy one of those jumpers shavers advertised on afternoon TV, I tried the lo-fi Sellotape method: snip a length of tape from the roll, apply sticky side to the jumper and peel back, which would do at a pinch, but doesn't stop the bobbling re-occurring.

So I reversed the jumper instead. I carefully unpicked the label and the care instructions (save this if you are forgetful of washing instructions) and the knit on that side was smooth and flat, and bobble free. And the side and shoulder seams look like carefully thought-out fashion details.

But sometimes things have gone beyond a bit of bobbling into disrepair . . .

How to DARN

In the olden days everyone had a darning mushroom to help them mend moth holes or a little wear and tear in their knitwear. You can invest in one from prickyourfinger.com. Or use a matchbox or your spare hand to gently stretch the area you're darning.

Thread your darning needle – it's a little longer than your regular needle – with thread that is the same colour and roughly the same weight as the holey garment.

Turn the garment inside out.

Anchor the thread in place with a few backstitches. Then sew some small running stitches around the hole. This will give the area a bit of extra strength and stop the hole getting bigger.

Spread the part that's going to be darned over the front of your fingers, the mushroom or the matchbox.

Sew a series of close-together, even stitches across the hole, but don't make them too tight as that will bunch up the fabric, too loose and everything will be floppy. They should look like the rungs on a tiny ladder.

Then begin weaving across the hole. Work at a right angle to the ladder stitches, and weave the needle and thread in and out of alternate rows of stitches, picking up the garment's fabric at each side, so that the hole is slowly closed over.

Finish the darning a little above the edge of the hole, so that it's all nice and secure and then do a few backstitches to prevent all your hard work unravelling.

Sometimes moth holes are pretty; their munching makes lacy patterns in the wool. To showcase this delicate look, blanket stitch around the holes, with fine, bright embroidery thread.

Or cut out little discs of lovely fabric and hand-sew them behind the holes. You can use running stitch, but blanket stitch would be just fine too.

SQUARE Lavender Bags

Wisdom has it that moths abhor strong smells, which was why mothballs, with their overpowering whiff of naphthalene, were supposed to do the trick. They may keep the moths away, but everyone else will be keeping their distance too. A sweeter way to prevent jumper feasts by wool-hungry moths is to put old-fashioned lavender or rosemary bags in with your knitwear. Even if they aren't as efficacious as mothballs, it's nicer to smell like a summer herbaceous border than a chemical spill. Little squares or rectangles are traditional for lavender bags but you could make them in any shapes you like – monsters, hearts, castles, birds, or, as my sister Una suggested, Lavender Old Bags, with a nod to our future.

Squares of COTTON FABRIC, 11CM X 11CM
DRIED LAVENDER FLOWERS *(I bought mine in
    Neal's Yard, where the herbs are stored in big
    old-fashioned jars)*
CARDBOARD, *or one of the take-away pizza
    menus that are piled up by the front door*

With the right sides together, sew around
three of the four square edges.

Do the same with the fourth side, but leave
A GAP of about 3cm

Flip the square right side out.

Make a little chute out of the pizza leaflet.
Use this to funnel the lavender flowers into
the square.

Sew up the 3cm gap.

The lavender scent will eventually fade;
to revitalise it, add a few drops of lavender
essence to the bag.

How to
SEW ON A PATCH

Moths aren't the only things that ravage a jumper. If, like me, you spend a lot of time leaning on your elbows, looking out the window, chances are that the holes on the elbows will be well beyond darning. So patch them instead. You can embrace the Seventies history professor look with fake suede or ploughed-field corduroy, but a pretty piece of fabric will be far lovelier.

Cut out an oval-shaped patch from your prettiest piece of material – about 4cm bigger than the elbow hole.

Cut ½ cm notches into the edges of the patch at 1cm intervals.

Pin the patch over the hole on the right side of the jumper, turning the notched edges under.

Sew the patch roughly in place with running stitches, ½ cm in from the edge, to keep it steady before you start the proper sewing.

With neat little stitches, sew the patch to your threadbare jumper.

Turn the jumper inside out, trim away the worn edge of the jumper – but don't cut into the patch.

Sew down the raw edges of the fabric patch to the jumper with tiny stitches, taking care not to stitch into the front of the patch.

Whip out any left over pins, and the tacking stitches.

A quick press with an iron will smooth out any wrinkles.

Customise your

If a plain jumper is looking a bit past its best,
or you're plain bored with it, you could:

ADD SOME SEQUINS

My friend Giles suggested 'You are dead to
me' picked out in Goth-coloured matte sequins
for a bit of dark glitter. I quite like the idea
of sewing 'Desperado' along the bottom of a
dark green jumper in pink, orange and blue
sequins for a take-no-prisoners colour scheme
and motif. And as a reminder of the dusky
days of autumn, stitch on handfuls of black
sequins to mimic a murmuration of starlings
wheeling against the sky of your pullover.

EMBROIDER A MESSAGE

Backstitch and embroidery-thread your
motto, mission statement or latest crush
onto the sleeves, along the hem, or proudly
flourish it across the back of your pullover.
Much less painful than a tattoo.

DECORATE WITH FLOWERS

The addition of a fabric flower pinned to
your shoulder will brighten up a dull jumper.
They are easy to make, and are a good way
of using up odds and ends of fabric.

knitwear

WORK SOME BUTTON MAGIC

Change the plastic buttons for fancy ones from your button jar. A proletarian black cardigan can be made fit for royalty with a pearly-queen make-over. You'll need a lot of buttons to be entirely regal, but a row of pearly whites sewed along the lapels and around the cuffs will cut a dash.

ADD STRIPS OF VELVET

Sew ribbons to the cuffs and edges of cardigans. Sewing the velvet to the outside will make it more luxurious, but if you sew secretive strips to the inside of the cardi's cuffs, it'll also feel lovely. There's nothing nicer than relishing a soft, glamorous texture against your skin while waiting at a rainy bus stop.

FABRIC Flowers

YOU'LL NEED:

ODDS *and ends of* FABRIC
SEQUINS
EMBROIDERY THREAD
SAFETY PIN *or a* **BROOCH BACK**
BUTTON
30CM X 20CM **THIN CARD**
FELT PEN
PAPER SCISSORS
NEEDLE & THREAD

Draw petal shapes onto the cardboard with the felt pen. Cut them out.

Use the template to cut out 12 petal shapes from the fabric.

With the wrong sides together, machine-sew two of the petal shapes together, using zigzag stitch.

Do the same thing with the rest of the fabric oddments.

Sew on some sequins and add some decorative embroidery thread stitches to your newly formed petals.

Hand-sew the six petals into a flower shape. And then add a button to the centre to finish your bloom off.

Attach a safety pin or sew a brooch back to your flower and then clip to the shoulder of your cardigan.

And finally...

Transform a Jumper into a GARDEN

I had a lovely old pale blue jumper, fine wool, with a round neck.
I also had a crush on hydrangeas: for years, I'd dismissed them as old-
ladies-swimming-cap flowers, and then suddenly I was smitten after
I saw a bunch of the dried blooms in the local florist. I bought a few cards
of slightly darker blue seam binding, gently gathered it, and then sewed
it around the yoke of the jumper. It looked just like a trim of unravelled
dried hydrangea petals.

And if it seems that your woolly really can't be saved, and you're tempted to discard it, don't. It can be cut up and transformed into Frankenstein creations, or felted in the washing machine. But those are wintry endeavours so fold them up, put them away with your lovely lavender bags, and forget about them until the evenings are long and the trees are bare.

I want outfits that would fit in with a nostalgic version of the SEASIDE...

I didn't spend a summer in the city until I was about 19. Up until then we all headed to Ireland for the six-week school holidays. When I was there I dressed in Jodie Foster *Freaky Friday* cords, a ragged T-shirt, bashed-up plimsolls, with barely brushed hair, and ran feral in the fields. I cycled up mad steep hills, so I could freewheel down the other side at top speed, trying not to snack on the clouds of midges that bounced up and down in the puddles, or breathe in the smell of dead badger in the undergrowth. And I never thought about what I was wearing, apart from one notable holiday where I pretty much spent every day in an old forest-green full-circle skirt of my mum's, from her dancing days, an orange tee with white lacing at the front, from my days as a pirate, a head-scarf and clogs. That was also the summer of eating pomegranate seeds with the point of a safety pin, and finger-length chunks of rhubarb dipped in paper cones of gritty sugar. I would like to claim that my summer wardrobe is inspired by these green-field memories – a dress woven from hay meadow flowers and a crown made from honeysuckle and dog roses, but instead thorny gorse (that smells of coconut) and woodbine hedges have (mostly) been replaced by the seaside.

A day out by the Atlantic had freezing sea, hot tea, and, if you were very lucky with the weather, hot sand. The dunes were lovely. Up in the scrubby grass, there were bright empty snail shells and butterflies, and if you laid back and pushed your fingers into the sand there, its temperature was always cool because the sun never reached that far. I'd like to have clothes that are the colour of those delicate snail shells, but also I want outfits that would fit in with a nostalgic version of the seaside, with an arcade, a bunting-bedecked pier, tap dancers and men with striped bathing suits and boaters.

I also want a Caftan...

Floaty, flimsy and nuanced with Sixties hippie deluxe glamour, the instructions are basically: sew two rectangles of nice fabric together, leaving a gap for your head. It's best to use fine, thin fabrics. Lovely lawn cotton or decoratively printed silk would be perfect, as would be transparent viscose. Avoid starchy fabrics – I tried to make one in crisp linen and I looked like an extra from *Battlestar Galactica*, rather than Talitha Getty on a Marrakesh rooftop.

This BILLOWY CAFTAN works best in gauzy fabric. It's big and loose, so if you want a bit of definition, buy some extra fabric – about 25cm – to make a sash, which you can tie around your waist, and flounce the excess material over it. Another 25cm will make a headscarf. Knot in under your hair, and let the ends trail over your shoulders.

YOU'LL NEED:
2 SQUARES *of* FABRIC 100CM X 100CM *(for a medium/large size)*
100CM *of* LOVELY RIBBON
MATCHING THREAD *(silk thread if you're using silk, cotton if you're making it in cotton)*

Zigzag the edges of the fabric to stop it fraying.

Fold one of the squares in half, and cut diagonally across one of the corners 15cm in from the top edge of the fabric, for the neck opening. Open the fabric back out into a square – it now has a perfect 'V' halfway along the top edge.

Lay it on top of the other square of fabric, right sides together. Sew along the shoulders, starting 20cm in from the outer edge on both sides.

Sew the side seams, starting 30cm down from the shoulder seams, and stopping 30cm from the bottom.

Turn a small hem under on the bottom edge, and along the side edges.

Sew the lovely ribbon around the 'V'-shape opening. It's quite nice to do this by hand with a needle and thread, but you can also use the machine.

The second caftan is FITTED –
two rows of side-stitching give
it shape and the shiny bells
give it rhythm.

YOU'LL NEED:
2 RECTANGLES *of* FABRIC 92CM X 95CM
MATCHING THREAD
80 – 100CM *of* SATIN BIAS BINDING
COLOURED BELLS *(optional)*

Zigzag the edges of the fabric to stop it fraying.

Fold one of the squares in half, and cut
diagonally across one of the corners 15cm in
from the top edge of the fabric, for the neck
opening. Open the fabric back out into a
square – it now has a perfect 'V' halfway
along the top edge.

Lay it on top of the other square of fabric, right
sides together. Sew along the shoulders, starting
20cm in from the outer edge on both sides.

25cm in from the side edges, and 30cm down
from the shoulder seams, sew the two rectangles
together to mid-thigh level.

Turn a small hem under on the bottom edge,
and along the side edges.

Sew the satin bias binding around the
'V'- shaped opening.

Hand-sew the shiny coloured bells around
the neck for a musical accompaniment to
your beach stroll.

BEACH BUNTING

Creating your own end-of-the-pier arcade might be tricky, but making the bunting to decorate it isn't. It's very easy, and by choosing jewel-bright colours and recycled fabrics with bold patterns and prints, you can add a bit of mix-and-match dash to your summer decorations. I made mine with furnishing fabric from Ikea, and different coloured strips of bias binding. The bunting can be bunged in the machine, on a cool wash, and restored to glowing summer brightness.

YOU'LL NEED:
1 *square of* STIFF CARD, 25CM X 23CM
A *selection of* FABRIC ODDMENTS, *large enough to cut into* 25CM X 25CM SQUARES
A *few cards of* BIAS BINDING, GARDEN TWINE *or* PIPING CORD
COLOURED PENCIL
RULER
SCISSORS
PINKING SHEARS
IRON
PINS

Mark out a triangle on the stiff card, with the felt pen and the ruler. The base of the triangle should be 23cm, and the two sides should measure 28cm.

Cut out the card triangle. This is the template for the bunting.

Using the template, draw lots of triangles on the wrong side of the fabric with the pencil.

Cut out the fabric triangles with the pinking shears.

Take two matching fabric triangles, and put them right sides together, and sew along the two long edges of the 'V' shape, about ½ cm in from the edge. Trim the fabric around the point of the triangle, close to the seam, but be careful not to cut into the stitches.

Turn the fabric triangle the right way out and iron it flat.

Turn in the base of the fabric triangle, and press with the iron.

Make a whole heap of these triangular pennants.

Pin the fabric pennants to the bias binding / garden twine / piping cord, then zigzag them in place with the sewing machine. You can let the triangles nestle against each other, or leave a gap between each fabric triangle, either way looks lovely.

Once you've mastered the technique, you can ring the changes and make bell-shaped bunting, bunting that looks like beach huts or sandcastles.

Or you can decorate your triangles with appliquéd fabric letters to spell out a motto – mine would be: Don't Forget The Factor Fifty (hot sun and pale skin = bad burns). You could also potato print or lino cut your own design before you make up the pennants, then sew silver bells onto the point for a little piece of chiming music in the summer breeze.

A Sunglasses Case

Bunting in hand, you can get on with making a beach bag, a sunglasses case, shorts and a sun hat that's big enough to fit a holiday donkey – essential things for a day at the beach.

YOU'LL NEED:
1 PIECE *of* FABRIC, 18CM X 20CM
1 PIECE *of* SOFT LINING FABRIC,
   18CM X 20CM *(you could use an old t-shirt)*
1 BUTTON
A *little twist of* FABRIC *to make a piece of piping for the button loop*
NEEDLE & THREAD

Take the fabric and fold it in half, right sides together. Sew up the side and along the bottom edge, close to the edge.

Turn the case the right way out and sew on the button, in the centre of the top edge and 2cm down from the top.

On the other side, sew on the piping loop
to match the position of the button.

Take the lining and fold it in half, right sides
together. Sew up the side and sew along the
bottom edge, but STOP 3cm from the end.

These next few steps are a bit mess-with-your-
mind. But it is a sewing trick of pure genius.
Slip the outside bit of the case inside the
lining. The outside should be the right way
out and the lining should be still inside out.

Sew the cases together, along the top edge,
as close to the edge as possible.

Pull the whole thing through the hole in the
lining. I know. But try it.

Hand-sew the gap in the lining, then gently
push the lining inside the case.

Ta da, a perfect finish, lovely and neat.

Now that you've worked that bit of
sewing magic, you can go to town on
the decorative front. Before you sew the
outside and the lining together, decorate
the outside with: appliquéd beach huts,
felt cupid kisses, ric-rac silver and
blue waves, a dash of white seagulls
embroidered with white thread, or back
stitch a motto with sparkly thread and
matte sequins.

A Reversible BEACH Bag

You'll need a bag to store all your beach paraphernalia.
This one is big and squashy and can fit a lot in. It's also
reversible, so it's two bags in one.

You'll need:

1 PIECE *of brightly patterned, fairly* HEFTY
COTTON, *or* THIN CANVAS, 56CM X 100CM

1 PIECE *of* BRIGHT FABRIC *in a different
pattern or in a* PLAIN BOLD COLOUR *in fairly*
HEFTY COTTON *or* THIN CANVAS, 56CM X
100CM

2 STRIPS OF CANVAS *or* COTTON,
14CM X 58CM, FOR THE HANDLES.
You could also use nylon webbing.

2 PIECES *of* MEDIUM-WEIGHT FUSIBLE
INTERFACING, 20CM X 56CM

IRON

Zigzag the edges of the fabric to prevent it
fraying.

Iron a strip of interfacing to the top edges of
the fabric on the wrong side.

Fold the first piece of fabric in half, widthways,
right sides together.

On the folded edge, at each corner, cut out a
square of fabric, 5cm x 5cm.

Sew the side edges together. But DON'T sew
around the bits where you cut out the squares.

Pinch those cut out corners together and sew
across them diagonally.

On the next piece of fabric, things are going to go just a little differently. For sewing purposes, this is going to be called the lining.

Sew up one of the sides.

Do the pinchy thing with both corners, and sew across them diagonally. Sew the last side but STOP, STOP, Stop about 6cm from the bottom of the bag.

If you are using webbing for the handles: fold the first strip in half lengthways, and sew along the side and both ends.

If you are using fabric for the handles: on the first piece of handle fabric, iron a strip of interfacing to the wrong side of the fabric to add a little extra strength.

Press a little hem on one of the width ends of the handles, onto the wrong side.

Fold the fabric in half, lengthways, right sides together, press with the iron, then sew along the 58cm length, and along one of the 14cm end, but not the other. Ironing before sewing helps to keep the handle on the straight and narrow.

Turn the handle the right way out. It may be a bit awkward, but persevere. Don't worry if it looks rumpled. A quick dash away with the smoothing iron will get those newly developed wrinkles out.

Sew that last end together. You can sew all around the handle if you fancy it, for a bit of extra decoration and strength.

Do the same thing with the other handle.

Turn the lining inside out.

Turn the other bag shape the right way out.

Pop the right-way-out bag into the inside-out-lining . . . it's just like the sunglasses case, the inside-out lining is on the outside, and the right-way-out bag is snug inside.

Sew them both together, close to the top edge.

Deep breath. Now gently pull the whole bag through that unsewn 6cm gap in the lining.

Sew up the gap, and neatly tuck the lining inside.

Sew on the fabric or webbing handles. It's a good idea to reinforce them by machine-stitching an 'X' shape for extra strength on the handle ends after you've sewn them to the bag.

You could add shorter handles to your seaside bag, as well as the over-the-shoulder option. Make them with smaller strips of fabric, or forage around a charity shop for something quirkier. I took apart an old wooden bead curtain tie back, re-strung the huge green beads onto two lengths of left-over felted wool (but piping cord would do be just fine too), for two carrying handles, and sewed them to the bag top. They make a nice abacus clicking sound when I'm walking across the sand.

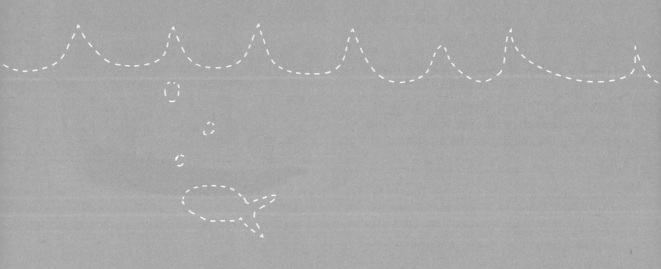

A Sun Hat

It's big and it's floppy and if you don't like it, you can give it to a passing holiday donkey.

YOU'LL NEED:
A PIECE *of* COTTON FABRIC,
    with a bold print, 80CM X 100CM
100CM *of* BIAS BINDING
A PIECE *of* LINING FABRIC, 30CM X 60CM
PINS
PAPER
PEN
COMPASS
PAPER SCISSORS
NEEDLE & THREAD
IRON

With a paper and pen, draw a circle, 15cm in diameter to make the crown pattern. Draw the side band on the paper, and draw the brim too:

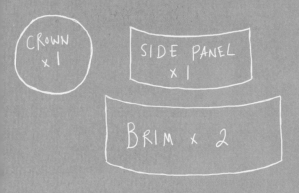

Pin the circle to the bold cotton. Cut out.

Fold the fabric in half, widthways, cut out one side band piece on the fold and two brim pieces also on the fold.

Zigzag the edges of the fabric.

With the right sides together, sew the side seam of the band piece.

With the right sides together, pin the side band to the circle crown. It should look like a fez, try it on, do a Tommy Cooper impression and then, just like that, get back to sewing the side panel to the crown.

With the right sides together, pin the brim pieces together, and then sew.

Notch the curved seam that you've just sewn (see page 22). Use a small pair of scissors, being careful not to snip into your stitches. Turn the brim the right way out.

Tack the inner edges of the brim together to keep the pieces aligned.

With the right sides together, pin the side band to the brim. Sew.

Hand-sew the bias binding to all the raw, tatty edges on the inside of the hat for a pretty finish.

To line the hat, cut out a crown piece and a side panel.

Zigzag the edges of the fabric.

With the right sides together, sew the side seam of the side panel.

With the right sides together, pin the side panel to the crown. Sew and then press a tiny hem to the wrong side of the fabric.

Leave the lining inside out and pop it inside the bold cotton hat. Hand-sew the lining to the brim, with small neat stitches.

EASY Summer SHORTS

YOU'LL NEED:

110CM X 150CM *of* SUMMERY FABRIC.
  Cotton would be lovely, but you could snip up last year's beach towel
110CM *of* ELASTIC *for the waist*
OLD PYJAMA BOTTOMS *to use as a pattern*
YOUR *faithful* QUICK UN-PICK
SCISSORS *for cutting paper*
SCISSORS *for cutting fabric*
2 SAFETY PINS
IRON
NEWSPAPER
FELT PEN
PINS

Try on your old pjs, and decide how short you want your shorts. Mark that length with a pin. Then add a second pin about 3cm down – these extra centimetres are for the hem.

Turn the bottoms inside out, and get busy with the quick unpick and undo the side seams on the inner legs, the centre seam, and the waistband (you could keep the elastic and use it for the shorts). Observe the weird shape of the taken-apart pjs. Who'd have thought that's what they'd look like flattened out? It might be a good plan to press the undone leg.

Make a pattern with the newspaper, felt pen and pjs. You only need to draw one leg. Before cutting the pj bottoms to make the shorts patterns, you might as well draw around the uncut leg… pyjamas bottoms are as easy to make as the shorts, you just need more fabric.

Pin the newspaper pattern to the folded fabric and carefully cut around pjs / pattern with the sharp dressmaking scissors. You now should have two weirdly shaped pieces of summer fabric.

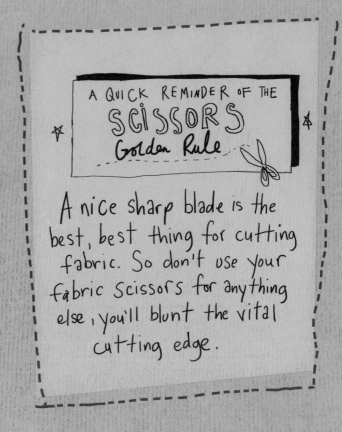

A QUICK REMINDER OF THE
SCISSORS
Golden Rule

A nice sharp blade is the best, best thing for cutting fabric. So don't use your fabric scissors for anything else, you'll blunt the vital cutting edge.

Zigzag the edges of the fabric to stop it fraying.

With the first leg, and with the right sides of the fabric together, sew the first inner seam – which is surprisingly small. Do the same with the second leg.

With the right sides together, pop one short leg inside the other, and pin the centre seam, then sew.

Now for the waistband. Your shorts should still be inside out.

Fold the waistband under 6mm and press.

Fold it over again, 2.5cm this time. Press.

This fold is going to be the casing for the elastic. So sew along the lower edge of that casing, but leave A GAP, so you can thread the elastic through.

Put the elastic around your waist. Note that measurement, then add another 5cm. Cut the elastic to that length.

Thread the elastic through the gap in the casing. I fastened safety pins to each end of the elastic, one I pinned to the shorts to stop the elastic getting lost in the casing, the other was a handy pulling tool for feeding the elastic through.

When it's all the way through, overlap the ends of the elastic, and safety-pin them together.

Try on the shorts and make sure the elastic is comfy. Whip the shorts back off if all is fine and dandy. (If not, loosen or tighten the elastic.)

Turn the shorts inside out and sew the overlapped ends of the elastic together. It might be a good idea to sew the elastic a couple of times to make sure it's good and secure.

Hand-stitch the gap in the casing, and distribute the gathers evenly along the waistband.

To stop the elastic runching up, head to the side seams of your shorts, and run a quick row of stitches through the waistband and into the side seams.

Do the hems on the legs of your shorts. Turn under 6mm and press. Turn under another 2cm, press, sew. Go for a paddle.

A CHIPFORK Necklace

There's nothing nicer than eating chips at the end of the pier, while keeping a weather eye on marauding seagulls. Don't throw away your chip forks, instead turn them into jewellery designed by GUEST STARS Rosie Wolfenden and Harriet Vine from super-cool jewellery label TATTY DEVINE.

YOU'LL NEED:

A HANDFUL *of* CHIP FORKS – *as many as you need to reach comfortably across your neck from one collarbone to the other*

6MM JUMP RINGS, *as many as you have chip forks (you may need some smaller ones if your chain has small links)*

ABOUT 20CM *of* CHAIN *(or an old necklace)*

1 CLASP *(a lobster clasp is best – this is the one that looks like a crustacean's claw – but any kind of clasp will do). Craft shops sell them*

MATT VARNISH

DRILL

2MM DRILL BIT

1 SCRAP PIECE OF FLAT WOOD *for drilling into*

WET AND DRY SAND PAPER, *which is very fine, and, as the name suggests, you can use it both wet and dry to get really smooth effects*

SMALL PAINTBRUSH

2 PAIRS *of* PLIERS

To get some wooden chip forks go to your local chippy, or perhaps take a day trip to the seaside if you don't have one nearby.

Placing the chip forks onto the scrap piece of wood, drill two holes in each fork at the rounded end. The holes need to be at least 2mm from the edge.

Give the chip forks a light rub with the sandpaper and wipe away any dust.

Varnish the chip forks all over, then leave them to dry.

When dry, rub the chip forks lightly with the sandpaper again. To get a really lovely finish, you can apply a second coat of varnish.

Once they are completely dry and smooth, link them together with the jump rings. Grip the jump ring with one pair of pliers, use the other pair to prise the jump ring apart. Attach as many as you need to reach comfortably across your neck from one collarbone to the other.

Using a jump ring, attach a 10cm length of chain to the last hole on the linked chip forks. Attach a lobster clasp to the other end of the chain.

Do the same on the other end of the chip forks, except finish off with a jump ring instead of the clasp.

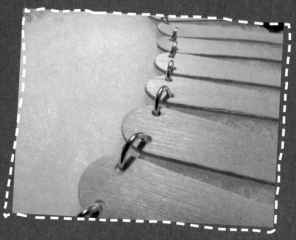

The length of chain is just a guide, and depends on the size of your neck and the amount of chip forks you use. It's best to start off with too much and shorten it as you need to, but try to keep the chain the same length each side.

The necklace looks great 'au naturelle', but would also look good painted with bright seaside colours or beach-hut pastels. You could also make matching sunglasses by gluing chip forks down the arms of your sunglasses!

A WEEK OF SUMMER TOPS

I love Fifties-style tops, the sort that can be worn with full circle skirts or pedal pushers by rockabilly girls who Lindy Hop on the weekends. They also look lovely with the beach shorts – you could make matching sets, for a perky Gidget look.

They take a couple of hours to sew, have a button at the back to fasten them and bust darts to add a little shape. They only use about 80-90cm of fabric, and are so easy to sew that you could run one up for everyday of the week. Make them in colours that have their own temperatures – warm yellow cotton, hot pink satin or cool white – and add on seven days of stand-out detail.

Top One
Plain and Simple

YOU'LL NEED
80CM-90CM *of* 150CM-WIDE FABRIC
1 CARD *of* 25MM BIAS BINDING
1 BUTTON
IRON
NEEDLE
THREAD

Cut out the fabric (see picture).

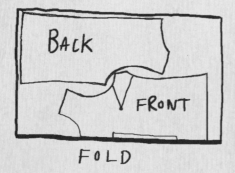

Zigzag the edges.

Sew the bust darts. Press them down.

With the right sides together, sew the two back pieces together up the centre seam. Stop 15cm from the top.

Press the seam open. Press the 15cm seams down, onto the wrong side of the fabric, then sew them individually. These make the back opening of the top.

With the right sides together, sew the shoulder seams.

Then sew the side seams, starting 8cm up from the bottom. These are going to be little side vents.

Press those little 8cm side vents and then sew them individually, not together.

Sew hems along the bottom.

Sew the bias binding around the neck, and the armholes. You can use the sewing machine, but it's one of the things I like to do by hand, there's something very soothing about it.

Make a thread loop, large enough for the button to pop through. Sew the loop to the neck of the top.

Sew on the button, on the opposite side to the loop.

Top Two
Sprinkled with Confetti

Four foraged, old-fashioned linen serviettes are perfect for this. Sew two of them together along their longest edges to make a square or rectangle, then do the same with the other two, and make up the top in the way described on page 95. With any left-over linen, cut out confetti petal pieces and stitch them to the top as if they'd been scattered there by the wind.

Top Three
Adorned with Pearls

Starched handkerchiefs would also make lovely tops. Collect a pile; wash well and then wash again, press and starch. Hand-sew on pearls saved from Christmas-cracker necklaces. That way, unlike Elizabeth I, you won't have to employ a pearl–picker-upper. Her gowns were so richly embellished with gems that her maids listened out for the distinctive sounds of the jewels detaching themselves and clickety-clacking to the floor.

Top Four
Made from Scarves

Charity-shop scarves would be beautiful, too. Use two scarves, with bold shapes or delicate patterns – one for the front and one for the back. If you are lucky enough to have found silk scarves use satin bias binding for the neck and arms. Cotton scarves will be perfectly complimented by cotton bias binding, in a matching or clashing colour. And for an extra decorative frisson, sew on beads or plastic jewels or glittery sequins.

Top Five
Decorated with Pom-poms

Even though you can easily rustle these tops up in 80cm of cloth, I always buy 100cm of fabric, and use the left-over pieces to make some added decoration.

FABRIC Pom-Poms

YOU'LL NEED:

LOTS *of* LEFT-OVER FABRIC *cut into thin strips*
1 SQUARE *of* CARDBOARD *(a square 8cm x 8cm will make a biggish pom-pom)*
TEACUP *(or a compass)*
PENCIL
QUICK UNPICK
SCISSORS

Draw two teacup circles onto the cardboard.

Draw two smaller circles in the middle of each of the bigger circles, using the bottom of the teacup or a compass, about half the size of your first circles.

Cut the big circles out, and then cut the smaller circles out.

Take a fabric strip and wind it around the cardboard, threading it through the middle circle, holding the end of the fabric against the cardboard with your finger and thumb, then working your way around the larger circle.

Do the same with the rest of the fabric strips until the big cardboard circle is covered, and the middle circle is practically filled in. Use the point of the quick unpick to pull the fabric through when the middle gets teensy.

Jab the point of the quick unpick in between the two covered circles, and saw through all the fabric layers.

Gently pull the two rings a little apart, and tie a fabric strip tightly between the two cardboard circles, leave a good dangling bit of fabric.

Ditch the cardboard circles and fluff up your pom-pom

You can make your pom-pom even more fancy – cut strips of fabric from scraps of brocade, or thin bits of Liberty print cotton will make a multi-coloured or glittery ball. They're perfect for using up odds and ends. Harvest those trimmed-off hems, seams and 'I'm just evening off this big ol' square' snippets and transform them into Pom-pom key-ring decorations, strung together as a necklace, a bracelet . . .

98

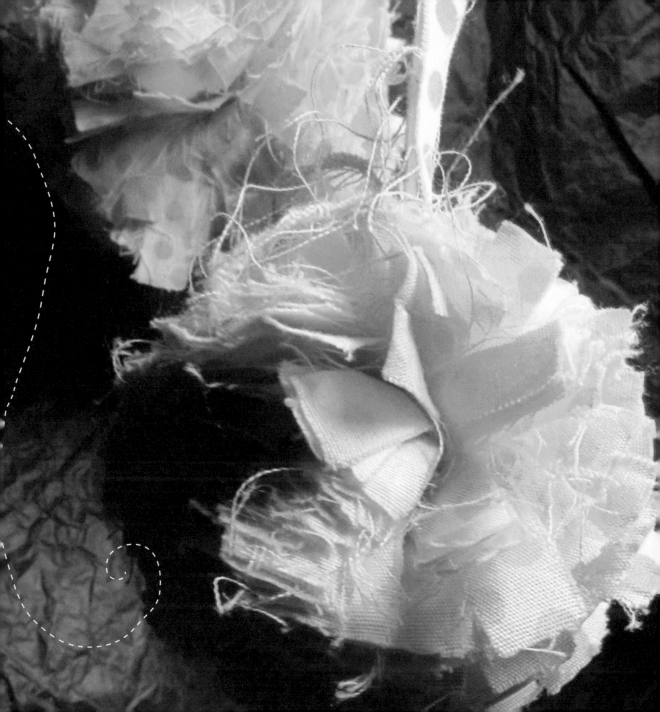

Top Six
Aflutter with Circles

You can use your cardboard circles as a template for circles of fabric. Make the top as in Top One. Then cut out circles of the same fabric, zigzag the edges of each disc to stop them fraying. And then hand-sew the circles onto the top with a few neat stitches at the top of the circles, overlapping them a little. You can also make scallop shapes and sew them on like fish scales.

Top Seven
'She was a Showgirl . . .'

I like a dilapidated edge to my satin summer tops. The look is easily achieved by ditching the bias binding and replacing it with un-hemmed strips of satin – the frayed edges look elegant and distressed, like an aristocratic show girl down on her luck. Wear powdery blue eyeshadow, the colour of mould, and suggestive of penicillin. And, in homage to Barry Manilow, a hair feather – attach with a clip, or sew a couple to a stretchy hairband and wear it across the forehead. Maybe avoid peacock feathers, as they are harbingers of doom.

You'll need:
1 strip *of* satin, 3cm x 40cm
Thread, matching *or* clashing, *the choice is yours*
Needle

Thread your needle with a long length of thread.

Anchor the thread with a backstitch just below the centre edge of the 3cm strip of satin.

Sew a line of running stitches along the length of the satin, slightly below the centre, leaving a tail of thread when you reach the end.

Sew a parallel line of running stitches along the length of the satin, slightly above the centre, leaving a tail of thread when you reach the end.

Gently pull the two threads to gather the fabric up. Even out the gathers, then anchor them with a backstitch.

Sew the gathers to the neckline of the top.

Drink Cava from a real champagne glass and bemoan the loss of your family's wealth to an unscrupulous fortune hunter with a waxed moustache.

SUMMER ISN'T SUMMER WITHOUT A DRESS OR TWO. HERE ARE THREE

A simple summer Dress

This dress, which is inspired by the paper frocks in the Victoria and Albert Museum, and one of Mia Farrow's frocks in *Rosemary's Baby*, has a simple, triangular shape, and is fairly short and I like it best made in crisp cotton, with a big bold print. It is VERY loose and perfect for throwing on on a sweltering day after a dip in the deep blue lido.

YOU'LL NEED:

1 PIECE *of* BOLD-PRINT COTTON, 150-170CM X 150CM
2 CARDS OF *matching or contrasting* BIAS BINDING
1 BUTTON
1 BUTTON LOOP
A VEST TOP *or* A SLEEVELESS DRESS *to use as a rough-and-ready template for the neck and armholes*
NEEDLE & THREAD
PINS
IRON
SEVERAL SHEETS *of* TAPED-TOGETHER NEWSPAPER *or* DRESSMAKER'S TRACING PAPER
FELT PEN
SCISSORS

Draw around the front of the dress, or vest. Draw around the back. Then draw the skirt bit.

Cut out the rough pattern pieces.

Pin the pieces together and try them on. See what you think. Keep cutting the paper until you're happy with the shape. Then make a new newspaper pattern with all the adjustments.

Fold your bold fabric in half. Put the pattern pieces on the fabric like this:

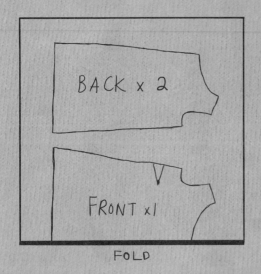

FOLD

Pin and cut.

Zigzag the edges of the fabric. Mark in the bust darts.

Stay-stitch the neck edges, and around the armholes.

Sew the bust darts. Press.

With the right sides of the fabric together, sew the shoulder seams. Press.

Sew the side seams. Press.

Sew the back together. But stop 30cm from the top. Press.

Turn those little side seams under. Press.

Hand-sew the bias binding around the neck edges, and the armholes. If you have enough binding, sew it to the little seams on the inside of the dress at the back.

Hand-sew the button on at the back.

Make a button loop, from a little piece of the bias binding.

Try the dress on and decide on the length. Sew the hem, and press.

OR you could add a zip, the instructions are much the same, except leave enough space in the back seam to put in a 30cm zipper. And you don't need the button and loop.

A PULL-OVER-YOUR-HEAD SUNDRESS

This dress is meant to be loose, and largely unfitted. It looks nicest with a belt fastened around the middle. Use one you already have, or skip to page 140 in Autumn.

YOU'LL NEED:
150CM *of* FABRIC
2 CARDS *of* BIAS BINDING
PAPER *and a* FELT PEN *to draw a rough pattern*
TAILOR'S CHALK
PINS
SCISSORS

Draw the pattern pieces and cut them out with any ol' scissors you like as long as they're NOT your fabric-cutting scissors.

Fold the fabric in half, right sides together.

Pin the pattern pieces to the fabric, like this:

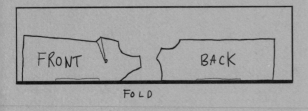

Mark the position of the bust darts onto the fabric with the pin and tailor's chalk method (see page 23). Cut.

Stay-stitch the neck edges, and around the armholes.

Zigzag the edges of the fabric.

Make the bust darts on the wrong side of the fabric. Press them to the centre.

With the right sides of the fabric together, sew the shoulder seams.

Sew the side seams. Press.

Try on the dress, and decide on the hem length. Sew the hem and press.

And you can add patch pockets too.

Cut out two squares of fabric. Zigzag the edges.

Press a skinny hem under on three sides of each of the squares of fabric. On each square on the un-pressed edge sew some pretty bias binging, in a matching or clashing colour.

Pin the pockets to the dress. Try the dress and on and see if the pockets are in the right place.

If they aren't, play around, until they are in just the right position for those summer sunshine, hands-in-pockets, slouchy moments.

If they are, sew around the three pressed sides. Don't sew the sides with the bias-binding trim or you will have two decorative squares rather than two handy pockets.

Add SCALLOPS to a Dress

A simple dress, like the one above, can be given a decorative edge with a scalloped hem. They are easy to make and seasidey on a cotton dress and medieval on a velvet one.

YOU'LL NEED:
EXTRA DRESS FABRIC *to make a facing for the scalloped hem*
CD
PAPER SCISSORS
PAPER
FELT PEN
PINS
NEEDLE & THREAD

Cut a strip of paper 10cm wide and half the length of the hem of your dress, plus 2cm, for the seams.

Use the curved edge of the CD to draw the scallops onto the strip of paper with the felt pen, like this.

Use paper scissors to cut around the curves.

Pin the scalloped strip to the ends of the dress pieces, and cut around the scalloped edges, so that your fabric is nicely scalloped.

Fold your strip of extra fabric in half, lengthways, and pin the paper strip along the fabric. Cut out carefully. You should now have two scalloped strips.

Zigzag the edges of the scalloped strips to stop them fraying.

With the right sides together pin the scalloped strip to the scalloped edges of the dress. Sew.

Clip the curves, being careful not to snip through your stitches – this will make those seams much less bulky. Press.

Hand-sew the facing to the inside of the frock, so that the stitches are practically invisible.

Gathered SUMMER DRESS

Sleeveless, with a back zip and a nicely gathered skirt, this is perfect to cut a dash on the dance floor.

YOU'LL NEED:
1 PIECE *of* FABRIC, 200CM X 150CM
1 ZIP, 55CM *long*
1 CARD *of* BIAS BINDING

Cut out the pattern pieces (see picture).

Zigzag the edges of all the pieces to stop them from fraying.

Stay-stitch the neck edges and around the arm holes.

Sew the waist darts on the wrong side of the front bodice. Press to the centre.

Sew the darts on each of the back bodice pieces. Press to the centre.

Gather the front of the skirt bodice. Even out the gathers so they are nicely spaced.

Gather the back two skirt pieces. Even them out too.

With the right sides together, sew the back bodice pieces to the back skirt pieces.

With the right sides together, sew the front bodice piece to the front skirt piece.

Starting from the bottom of the back of the dress, and with the right sides still together, sew the back pieces together. STOP 56cm from the top

Put the zip in that 56cm gap.

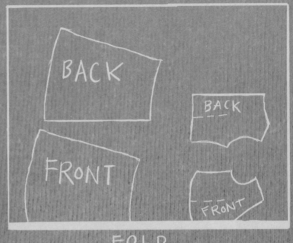

With the right side together, sew the back and front of the dress together across the shoulders. Press.

Now sew up the side seams. Press.

Stitch the bias binding around the neck, and the armholes.

Go dancing with someone wildly inappropriate.

To make the dress extra pretty you could sew a line of seashells across the bodice. Or make a garland of fabric flowers to decorate the neckline.

A FLOWER

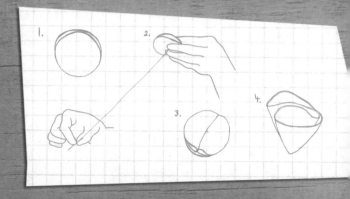

to GRACE the NECK of your DRES

YOU'LL NEED:
A STRIP *of* FABRIC *approx* 20CM X 40CM
CARDBOARD, *approx* 10CM X 10CM
PENCIL
A BIG MUG
NEEDLE & THREAD
SCISSORS
SPRAY STARCH *(entirely optional)*

Put the mug onto the cardboard and draw around it. Make sure the mug is empty before you start, to avoid accidents with hot beverages and pretty fabrics.

Cut out the cardboard circle. Use it as a template and draw 16 circles onto the fabric. (You can, of course, skip this stage and just draw around the mug.)

Cut out the 16 fabric circles.

Hand-sew the first two circles together.

Fold the next four circles in half, and hand-sew them (see pic), with a few little stitches at the centre to anchor them in place.

Fold the eight remaining circles into four, and hand-sew them (see pic), with their pointy ends at the centre of the circle.

Fluff up the petals.

Spritz with some spray starch for an upright look.

Hand-sew to the neck of the dress.

Admire your work. Make a lot more flowers and it'll look even nicer. To make a fuller flower, cut more circles, fold them into four, and hand sew to your burgeoning flower.

little Edie

+ HER REVOLUTIONARY COSTUME

OR

HOW GEOMETRY MAKES NICE CLOTHES

I am always on the look out for people with resourceful ideas for their wardrobes, which I can then try to use in mine. Little Edie Bouvier, the star of the Maysles' documentary *Grey Gardens* was a 'staunch woman' who lived in a ramshackle mansion in East Hampton, Long Island, from the early Fifties until 1979. She shared the house with her mother, a collection of cats and some burglar racoons. Although related to Jackie O, the pair fell on straightened times, but remained eccentrically undaunted – 'I'm a marvellous specimen, and so is my mother. And we live on practically nothing.' Edie invented a revolutionary costume – a cardigan wrapped around her head and secured with a huge brooch and a skirt made of a rectangle of fabric knotted at the waist, and pinned, like a kilt, with a safety pin. 'You can always take the skirt and use it as a cape . . . so I think this is the best costume for the day.'

And it's true, squares and rectangles make nice clothes. Even Art Deco couturier Paul Poiret would agree. He made a lovely dress, based on a deconstructed kimono – constructed from egg-yolk-yellow wool, with black-chiffon lining. It was two rectangles folded on the shoulders, with one side caught up with a huge bow, and that was it. Not everyone was a fan of his imaginative geometrical thinking. Hamish Bowles, in '*Fashioning the Century*', described Russian Princess Baraintinsky's reaction to Poiret's present of a Confucius coat thus: 'What a horror. When there are low fellows who run after our sledges and annoy us, we have their heads cut off and we put them in sacks just like that.' So here are a few things inspired by rectangles, Edie and Mister P, but without the threat of algebra, cat invasion or injury by émigrée princesses.

"what a horror. When there are low fellows who run after our sledges and annoy us, we have their heads cut off and we put them in sacks just like that."

Elizabeth's SILK top

80cm of printed silk will make a sweet, pull-over-the-head top. Or you could buy strips of jewel-coloured silk satin, cut them into geometrical shapes and sew them together in patterns inspired by kaleidoscopes.

My friend Elizabeth, who likes order better than chaos, made a startling slash-neck top, in electric blue and chocolate brown – with a flash of shocking pink where she ran out of the other two shades – in neatly aligned steps of silk. She cut them into rectangles, then sewed them together, with silk thread and very narrow seams, pressing everything flat as she went.

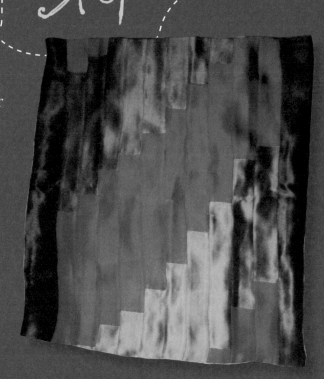

YOU'LL NEED:
1 PIECE *of* SILK, 40CM X 115CM
1 PIECE *of* SILK *of a different colour*,
   40CM X 115CM
SILK THREAD
2 SQUARES OF 50CM X 50CM *of* LIGHT FABRIC
   for lining (optional)
50CM X 50CM *of* BLANK PAPER,
   or A SHEET *of a* NEWSPAPER
SCISSORS
RULER *and* PENCIL

Cut strips of 20cm x 5cm of two different coloured silks.

Press them until they are wrinkle free.

Take a strip of each colour and, with the right sides together, sew them along one of the small edges.

Then, still with the right sides together, sew a third strip of silk to the other small edge.

The aim is to have a long strip of fabric about 2m long, made up of alternating colours.

Press all the seams flat and open.

Cut out a 50cm square of blank paper or newsprint. This is the size that your top is going to be, and the silk strip is going to be cut into smaller strips to form a pattern of your choosing.

Lay the silk strip onto the paper, and have a think, before you start to cut. Folding the fabric to see what looks best, you could organise it horizontally or vertically or diagonally. Elizabeth chose vertical, with a rising, stepping pattern.

Mark the square to show where your strips will be placed with a pencil and ruler and then lay the long strips over the marks, cutting it into the sections that you need to follow your chosen pattern. You'll begin to see the pattern forming as you lay your strips onto your paper grid.

Make more 2m strips as you need them.

When all the strips are in place on the square, start sewing them together with long, straight seams, and always with the right sides together.

Press the seams at the back so that they're nice and flat. This square is the front.

Make another square for the back. If you want, you could make the pattern 'connect' interestingly at either side – or you can just let the front and backs be different. If you're all matched out, the back could also be un-patterned – a single square of coloured fabric will do the trick.

When the two squares are done, with the right sides together, sew the shoulders, leaving room for your head.

With the right sides together, sew the side seams. Leave room for your arms. You can line the neck and armholes, or, if you use silk, you can singe the edges with a lighter – but make sure you don't singe your seams because it will all fall apart. And be careful with the flame, otherwise you are in grave danger of burning a big old hole in the top. A single coloured silk top in dove grey, shadowy black or old parchment brown, made as a square and with singed edges would be particularly nice.

OR

You could line each silk square by sewing it right sides together to a piece of light lining fabric on three of the sides. Turn them the right way out and press. The unsewn edge is the bottom of the top.

Pin the sides together from the bottom of the top to the armhole, and hand-sew the sides together from between the linings using tiny slipstitches, which will be practically invisible.

Slipstitch the shoulder seams too.

Equally simple, and as dramatic, was the expensive designer

dress that I tried on in a boutique with velvet curtains and a

wooden floor painted white. It was very simple and very lovely,

made from a double-ended zip and a wisp of very expensive

silk. The zip ran from shoulder to shoulder, and the silk, which

tapered to the knees, was sewn to the zip. Trying on a dress

like that is always a dangerous thing: like kissing someone

inappropriate, it can lead to heartbreak and cut-up credit cards.

To save myself from that dastardly fate, I made my own version

with thin cotton and a zip foraged from my brother's old fleece.

But you can also buy zips by the metre, it's usually one zip per

50cm, so you'll need 100cm.

A ZIPPED Shoulder Dress

YOU'LL NEED:
1 DOUBLE-ENDED ZIP, 55CM *long*
1 PIECE *of* THIN COTTON, 110CM X 150CM

Cut the cotton into two equal rectangles, 55cm x 150cm.

Zigzag the edges.

Sew the rectangles to the zip.

With the right sides together, sew the side seams. Stop 22cm from the zip top – these are the armholes.

Try on the dress, and decide on the length. Cut to fit and then sew a hem.

As an alternative to the 55cm zip, you can use 2 x 25cm zips, which are much cheaper. Make much the same way, but with the zips at either end of the fabric, and a gap in the middle for your swan neck to slink through.

A little top using the zip idea would be a lovely thing to make, too, in midnight blue, zingy lime green or a clashy turquoise silk. To stop the silk slipping about when you're cutting it out, put an old sheet, or some cotton under the fine fabric before you get busy with the scissors. And use silk thread too. And if you want a really professional look, slide tissue paper between the seams as you sew, this will stop the silk from puckering. When you've finished sewing, gently tear the tissue paper away.

little BITS & PIECES

TO CHEER YOU UP WHEN YOU'RE FEELING SHORT-CHANGED

A PURSE THAT'S LIKE AN ENVELOPE

This purse is perfect for using up left-over fabric. Or treat yourself to a small bit of something glittery and expensive.

YOU'LL NEED:
A RECTANGLE *of* FABRIC, 30CM X 15CM
A RECTANGLE *of* LINING FABRIC,
    30CM X 15CM
MATCHING THREAD
2 SNAP FASTENERS
A BUTTON *or* TWO (*optional*)

Put the right sides of the fabric rectangles together.

Stitch around the edges. But leave a 4cm gap on one of the sides.

Turn the potential purse the right way out, through the gap.

Close the gap with a few quick stitches.

Make a purse shape by folding 26cm of the 30cm in half to make a 13cm pocket. The remaining 4cm is going to be the flap.

Sew up those 13cm sides.

To achieve closure, sew on the snap fasteners.

And add a button or two for decoration.

A Butterfly Hairband

You'll need:
A Plastic *or* Metal Hairband
A Selection *of* Paper Butterflies
Millinery Wire
Strong Glue
Sharp Scissors

Snip the millinery wire to various lengths.

Carefully glue the fragile paper butterflies to one end of each strand of millinery wire.

Twist the other ends of the millinery wire around the hairband, so that the butterflies look like they are dancing above your head.

I love it when the air smells of smoke, and it makes me wish my clothes had the delicious scent of burning leaves and chestnuts....

Although it is tempting, on the damper days of autumn, to stay indoors and daydream of boys with melancholy fringes who spend their evenings drawing portraits of shadows, a little trip out to the park is always good for the spirits. Especially when the park is full of crunchy leaves and the air smells of kindling wood. I love it when the air smells of smoke, and it makes me wish that my clothes had the delicious scent of burning leaves and roasted chestnuts. It would be nice to kipper them in some handy chimney and pull them out, a little sooty, but smelling of bonfires and braziers. But if I can't do that, I can have smoke-coloured clothes. A purchase of some dark-grey felted wool a while back means that I can have a dress (made from a bought pattern) spray painted in shades of gold, pink and blue flame, with a dabbed splash of Comme des Garcons 2 Man perfume at the wrist, which is as fragrant as tapering candle smoke. I also made a little grey capelet and a collection of ornamental collars, one sewn with sequins the colours of dewy leaves, hedgerow hips and scarlet berries. And there's even enough wool left over to make a big tote, sewn with a web of silvery beads, with a spider in the middle, just like the ones which suddenly appear everywhere in September and October and then disappear again. Except my spider is plastic. And as the weather is getting chilly, grey woolly socks are the order of the day, with garters that sparkle with stars and moons.

It's also tempting to wear dresses that are as stark as Penelope Tree's Halloween Ballet costume, in colours that would garner me an automatic invite to Truman Capote's black-and-white masked ball, but I always remind myself not to ditch bright shades for the lure of monochrome. A skirt as orange as a harvest pumpkin, a bold red vinyl bag dangling with a pound-shop skeleton and maybe a clutch of skulls in celebration of the Mexican Day of the Dead is what I should favour.

And every year, I think about making an acorn necklace, helicopter earrings and conker buttons and wish that I had a crown made from the antlers of branches, and a cloak made of leaves, and cheeks as pink as sloe gin. So far I haven't made the conker necklace, but I have made a dress that's forest green and developed a crush on guest star Alison Wonderland's padded camera bag, which is printed to look just like a camera.

125

TOTE BAG

decorated with a spider's web

It's one of the first things I say in September: 'The Spiders Are Back.' Before I say that, I am largely silent, and sewing a lot of beads onto a bag decorated with a spider.

YOU'LL NEED:

1 PIECE *of* FELTED *or* BOILED WOOL, 43CM X 43CM, *for the bag (you can make the bag bigger or smaller)*

1 PIECE *of* FABRIC, 43CM X 43CM, *for the lining*

2 STRIPS *of* MEDIUM WEIGHT FUSIBLE INTERFACING 43CM X 12CM

2 STRIPS *of* FABRIC 60CM X 10CM *for the handles (or you could use 2 strips of webbing, 60cm x 5cm)*

LONG SILVER BEADS

SILVER SEQUINS *(optional)*

1 SPIDER

BEADING THREAD

BEADING NEEDLE

IRON

TAILOR'S CHALK

GLUE

...on the interfacing to the wrong sides of the top edges of the felted wool.

Draw a spider's web pattern onto the right side of one of the pieces of felted wool with tailor's chalk. Pick out the web's strands with the silver beads, using the beading needle and beading thread.

Hand-sew, or glue, a spider into the middle of the web.

A silver sequin border will look fetching stitched around the bag's edge. Hand-sew the sequins in from the edge so that they don't get lost when you sew up the bag's sides. If you've enough sequins, you can add a border to the un-cobwebbed piece of fabric.

With the right sides together, sew the sides seams and across the base.

Make the handles. Fold one strip of 60cm x 10cm fabric in half lengthways. Press and sew.

Do the same with the other strip of fabric.

Pin and sew to the bag.

Zigzag the edges of the lining.

With the right sides together, sew the side seams and along the base.

Press a tiny hem under the wrong side of the lining. Pop the lining inside the bag, and sew as close to the top edge as possible. Don't accidentally sew the handles out of kilter.

A RED vinyl bag

One of my favourite shops is the Japanese sock store Tabio, which sells tights in electrifying colours. I have a cash limit, no-credit-card policy when I saunter in there, otherwise bankruptcy would beckon. This juicy-red vinyl bag is inspired by their scarlet tights. I've added an optional skeleton.

YOU'LL NEED:
2 PIECES *of* STIFF VINYL FABRIC, 45CM X 50CM
2 PIECES *of* STIFF VINYL, 8CM X 50CM
2 PIECES *of* LINING FABRIC, 45CM X 50CM
1 GIANT ZIP
1 D-RING *or piece of* RIBBON
1 TOY PLASTIC SKELETON
LEATHER NEEDLE *for the sewing machine*
RULER
TAILOR'S CHALK
PINS
NEEDLE & THREAD
IRON

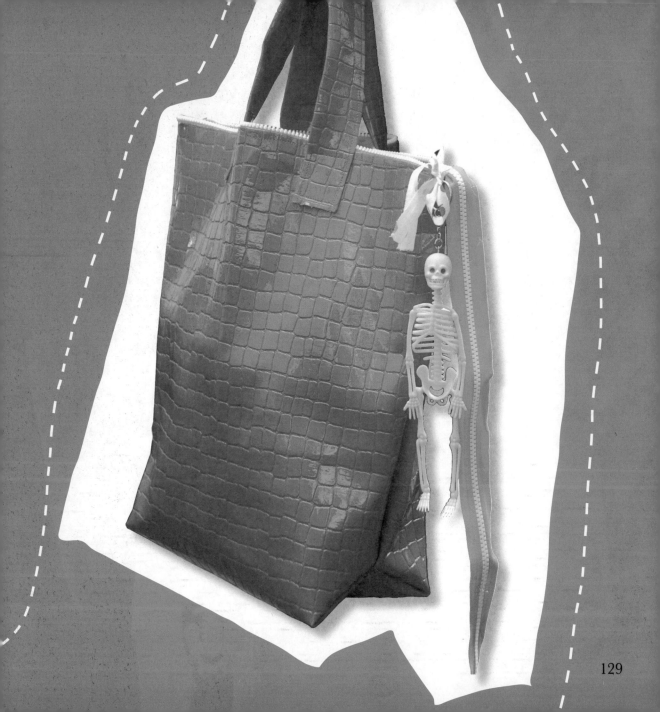

Swap the ordinary machine needle for the leather needle.

On the bottom corner edges of the vinyl fabric, cut out a rectangle 10cm long, 5cm wide.

Do the same with the bottom corners of the lining fabric.

On the top edges of the vinyl fabric, turn a 3cm hem to the wrong side of the vinyl. Sew.

Sew the giant zip to the top edges of your yet unformed bag. Unzip the zip.

With the right sides together, sew the side seams, but not the cut-out corners, of the vinyl fabric.

Now sew along the bottom edge.

Pinch the corners, and sew across them diagonally.

Trim the corners, being careful not to snip into the stitches.

Turn the bag the right way out through the open zip.

With the wrong sides together, fold the first vinyl strip, 8cm x 50cm, in half lengthways. Sew around the edges.

Do the same with the second vinyl strip, 8cm x 50cm. These are the handles.

Pin the handles to the outside of the bag, and then sew.

Swap the leather needle for the ordinary machine needle and zigzag the edges of the lining fabric.

Press a 3cm hem to the tops of the lining fabric.

With the right sides together, sew the side seams, but not the cut-out corners. And then go ahead and sew along the bottom.

Pinch the corners, and sew across them diagonally.

Trim the corners, being careful not to snip into the stitches.

Leaving the lining inside out, pop it inside the bag.

Swap the ordinary needle for the leather needle on the machine and sew the lining neatly in place. Carefully sew the lining to the interior of the bag.

With the D ring, or the ribbon, attach the skeleton to the zipper bit of the giant zip.

Head to Tabio, on the Mexican Day of the Dead, to buy three pairs of new poppy red tights to match your bonny, bony new bag.

A *leather* BAG

I love the way Edith Evans, as Lady Augusta Bracknell, says 'A HANDBAG' in the 1952 film of *The Importance of Being Earnest*. This leather bag, made from an old leather jacket, is big enough for a baby or a hefty manuscript. There was still enough leather left over to make a decorative bag charm. If you're not keen on using recycled leather, wet-look vinyl would look pretty fine, too.

YOU'LL NEED:

A LARGE LEATHER JACKET *or* COAT
  (or, whisper it, leather trousers)
If you are going to make the bag in a FABRIC
  other than leather, have TWO PIECES *of*
  FABRIC 55CM X 45CM *to hand*
2 PIECES OF FABRIC, 55CM X 45CM,
  for the lining
55CM ZIP
2 STRIPS OF LEATHER, 10CM X 10CM
2 D-RINGS
2 DOG LEADS
NEEDLE & THREAD
ZIPPER FOOT *for the sewing machine*
LEATHER NEEDLE *for the sewing machine*

If you're recycling a jacket or coat, cut two rectangles measuring 55cm x 45cm from the body of the garment. While you are at it, salvage the zip, or buttons and save the left over leather.

Change the ordinary sewing machine needle for one that can deal with leather. Leather can be tough to sew and can snap an everyday machine needle.

With the right sides together, tack the leather pieces along one long side.

Centre the closed zip on the underside of that seam and tack in place.

Sew the zip in.

Open the zip half way. If you don't do this now, there will be trouble later.

With the right sides of the leather together, sew the side seams. (If you say that instruction out loud it sounds like a song from *Sesame Street*).

Sew along the bottom.

Turn the bag the right way out through the open zip.

Fold the 10cm x 10cm leather strips in half, and stitch around the edges.

On each of the strips, thread a D-ring.

Loop the leather strips with the D-rings to each side of the bag and hand-sew in place.

Zigzag the edges of the lining fabric.

Press tiny hems onto the wrong sides of the top edge.

Pop the lining inside the bag. Machine stitch it to the leather bag, just below the zipper.

Attach the dog leads to the D-rings. These are the bag's shoulder strap.

A TELLY Bag Charm

Time to retire to the sofa, settle down and watch TV, and use the left-over leather to make this brilliant Telly Charm for your bag, designed by GUEST STAR Zoe Larkins, accessories designer and Monster Maker of super-cool label Love From Hetty and Dave (www.lovefromhettyanddave.co.uk).

YOU'LL NEED:

1 PHOTO-BOOTH PIC *of you with your best friend, or your pet cat or a scarecrow that looked lonely in a bare, harvested wheat field*

1 KEY RING

3 RECTANGLES *of* BLACK LEATHER 8CM X 6CM

1 STRIP *of* BLACK LEATHER, 1CM X 4CM

1 *small scrap of* SILVER LEATHER *to cut out the tiny telly knobs and switches, the trim, and the vintage telly details*

1 SQUARE *of* CLEAR PLASTIC, 5CM X 4.5CM *(You could use the front of a Tunnock's tea-cake packet, and then use the rest of the box to make a mini theatre, with a castle backdrop and haunted woods scenery inspired by Joseph Cornell's 'Setting for a Fairytale')*

1 STIFF PIECE *of* CARD, 8CM X 6CM

SCISSORS

GLUE

NEEDLE & THREAD

Cut out a square in one of your leather rectangles for the telly screen and glue clear plastic onto the back, so you have a window.

Glue on the silver knobs, the on-switch, and the trim – which goes around the screen.

Add a few hand-stitched details on the knobs and switch for some vintage authenticity.

Next, fold the 1cm x 4cm black leather strip in half, widthways, and thread it through the key ring.

Put a blob of glue on the wrong side of the leather strip and carefully squish the two sides together.

Put the stiff card between the two remaining rectangles, wrong sides together, and place the end of the leather strip with the dangling key ring at the top and glue everything together. Make double sure that the right sides face out.

Add some hand stitches to keep the key ring securely in place

Glue the very outer edge of the telly face onto the sandwiched rectangle pieces, but remember (!) to leave the top part unglued to slide in the pic of your choice.

And finally hand-stitch around the sides for that finishing touch.

A FORAGED CHINA
NECKLACE + Charm Bracelet

I always like the idea of transforming throwaway things into something else entirely. (Sometimes I have to mutter a reminder to myself: 'Not everything needs to be made into something else'). Lighting designer Stuart Haygarth can work spells with the trashy stuff of modern life and magic them into something lovely. He has created a series of Tide Chandeliers, with strung-together plastic debris that he found washed up on the Kentish coast. He's made optical lights from the unwanted lenses of abandoned reading glasses, from recycled bottles, old car tail lights, and with 1,000 exploded party poppers picked up after the London Millennium celebrations. On my walks in the park I tried to see the world through Stuart Haygarth's eyes and collected pieces of smashed blue and white china that appeared in the paths after the rain, washed them and made them into a necklace and a little china charm bracelet.

Assemble your china pieces.

Assemble your jump rings.

Make sure your china is clean, otherwise the glue might not glue.

Glue the jump rings to the unpatterned side of the china, behind the top edge, making sure the rings peek over the top of the china.

Wait for the glue to dry and then wait some more.

Prise open the unused jump rings with the pliers. This can be tricky, so have a cache of creative swear words at the ready.

Loop these jump rings through the jump rings on the china, and then through the chain.

Close the jump rings with the pliers.

Attach the clasp with the pliers.

Make a charming bracelet to match in exactly the same way, but with a smaller chain.

YOU'LL NEED:
BROKEN CHINA
A LENGTH *of* CHAIN, *which you can buy at craft shops or* AN OLD NECKLACE.
BIG JUMP RINGS
A CLASP
A PAIR *of* PLIERS
VERY STRONG GLUE

A CHINA BROOCH

You can add a brooch to your china set. This takes no time at all to make but it might take you a while to spot a pretty piece of broken china.

NO NEEDLES!

YOU'LL NEED:
1 *bigger piece of* BROKEN CHINA
1 BROOCH BACK
GLUE

Open the brooch back. Glue the brooch back to the china.

Wait for it to dry.

A LEGO
BELT BUCKLE

You can make your own belt buckle and not rely on one purloined from your sister's coat. I once had a Saturday job where, for about eight hours a day, I tidied up the Lego; it was strangely hypnotic. Just wearing this belt buckle is liable to send me into a trance.

YOU'LL NEED:
LEGO!

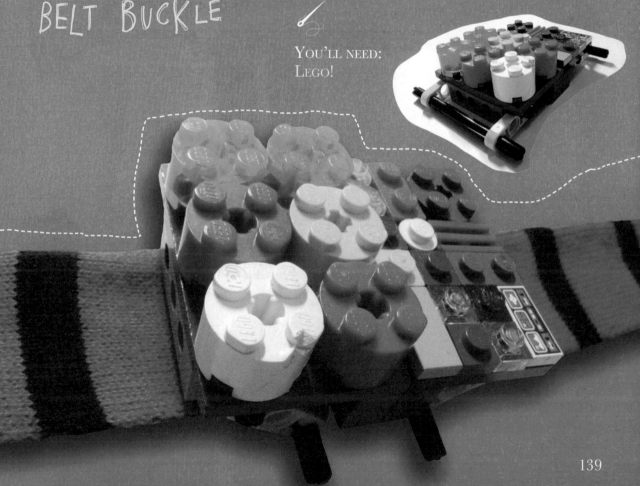

A Quick Belt

I always have long strips of
fabric lying around. Here's an easy-
to-make belt made up of a piece
of cut-up upholstery fabric in
colours guaranteed to chase
away autumn clouds.

YOU'LL NEED:

1 THREAD-THROUGH BELT BUCKLE
(don't use a pronged one, unless you are
the proud owner of an eyelet kit)

1 STRIP OF FABRIC, AT LEAST 115CM LONG
(the width of your fabric depends on the size
of the buckle. Measure the bit where you're
going to thread the belt fabric through. Note
that measurement, double it and then add
another centimetre)

MEDIUM-WEIGHT FUSIBLE INTERFACING,
the same length as the belt fabric, but half
the width

A FEW LITTLE LEFT-OVER BITS of NARROW
BIAS BINDING for the belt loops

IRON

A BIG SAFETY PIN

Zigzag the edges of the fabric.

With the right sides together, fold the fabric
in half, lengthways and press.

On the wrong side of one half of the folded
fabric, iron on the long strip of medium-
weight fusible interfacing.

With the right sides together, and with the
fabric still folded in half, whiz a ½ cm seam
around the belt. Do sew one of the skinny
ends. DON'T sew the other skinny little end.

Trim the end of the belt by cutting the corners
on the diagonal, be careful not to snip your
stitches.

Here is a moment where you might wish
you had a better equipped sewing tin. Phil
Davison, who runs the craft label Urban Cross
Stitch (his street-art-inspired kits make proper
ladies blanch at sewing exhibitions), spent one
evening turning 100 handles for 50 tote bags,
using the big safety-pin method, while pining
for a Rouleau loop turner. This handy little
gadget is a long length of fine metal, with a
latch hook on the end, and is made for turning
narrow tubes of fabric the right way out.
He said it would be worth £2.50 of anyone's
money. I don't have one, so think of snakes
shedding their skin, attach the big safety pin
to the end of the fabric and wriggle the belt
until the wrong side is inside and the right side
is outside.

Tuck the unsewn ends of the belt inside and
neatly sew.

Loop one end of the belt through the middle of
the buckle, with an overlap of 5cm. Sew.

To make the belt loops, grab the snippets of
narrow bias binding, and with the right sides
together, sew it into circles. Turn the circle the
right way out and then slide them onto the
belt.

A Guesswork DIRNDL SKIRT

This skirt sounds like it belongs in an old-fashioned version of the Swiss Alps. It is softly gathered, but if you use a retro print the dirndl will look like a vintage skirt from the Fifties.

There's probably a seamstresssy way of making this skirt so that the finish is couture, but I made it up as I went along, and it worked out pretty fine. First up, I measured my waist, and then added a few centimetres to that number to allow for a side seam. I went for a skinny waistband – about 10cm wide.

I knew I was going to use two rectangles of fabric for the skirt bit, so I measured my hips and added on an extra 40cm for each rectangle. Then I roughly measured from my waist to my knee and added on a good few extra centimetres to get the length, plus hems, plus wonky cutting.

YOU'LL NEED:

2 RECTANGLES *of* FABRIC FOR THE SKIRT
  (see above)
1 LONG THIN RECTANGLE *of* FABRIC *for the*
  waistband (again see above)
MEDIUM WEIGHT FUSIBLE INTERFACING *for the*
  waistband
1 ZIP, 20CM LONG
PINS
NEEDLE & THREAD

Zigzag the fabric rectangles.

Zigzag the edges of the waistband.

Gather the fabric, either by hand: stitch two
parallel rows of running stitch along the top
edge of the first piece of fabric. Or by machine:
adjust the stitch length – set it to longest
length, and loosen the stitch tension, then sew
two parallel rows of stitches along the top edge
of the first piece of fabric.

Do the same with the second piece of fabric.

Pull on either end of the threads to gather the
fabric up.

With the right sides together, sew one of the
skirt side seams all the way from the top to
the bottom.

With the right sides together, sew the other
side seam but stop 16cm from the top. This is
where the zip is going to go.

Even out the gathers until the skirt is roughly
the same size as the waistband.

To make the waistband, there's going to be a
bit of hand sewing and a bit of machine work.

First iron the interfacing to the wrong side of
the waistband. Press a skinny hem under the
thin ends of the waistband.

With the right sides together, pin one long edge
of the waistband to the gathered waist of the
skirt. Have another check to see if the gathers
are fairly evenly spaced. If you're happy, go
ahead and sew.

Press a skinny hem under the other long
waistband edge.

Fold the waistband over and then hand-sew
this just-pressed long edge to the inside of
the skirt. Press again for neatness sake.

Put the zip in.

Try the skirt on and decide on the length.
Cut with confidence.

Press a skinny hem on the bottom edge of the
skirt. Press under a further 1cm and then sew.

143

A Guesswork ROUGHLY PLEATED SKIRT

I wanted a skirt that was a little like a bell. So instead of using the fine cotton of the Guesswork Dirndl, I picked starchy cotton that would hold its shape. And I did away with the gathers, and went for rough pleats instead, but the measurements and the method are pretty much the same.

YOU'LL NEED:
2 RECTANGLES *of* FABRIC FOR THE SKIRT *(see p.142)*
1 LONG THIN RECTANGLE *of* FABRIC *for the* WAISTBAND *(again see p.142)*
MEDIUM WEIGHT FUSIBLE INTERFACING *for the waistband*
1 ZIP, 20CM LONG
PINS
NEEDLE & THREAD

Zigzag the fabric rectangles.

Zigzag the edges of the waistband.

With the right sides together, sew up one of the side seams.

Then sew the other, but stop 16cm from the top. This is where the zip is going to go.

Now for the pleats. You don't have to be stunningly accurate, use the waistband strip as a guideline, and fold the fabric in the way you would if you were making a giant paper fan. Pin the pleats as you go, so you can see how things are panning out, and remember that the skirt should roughly match the waistband.

Iron the interfacing to the wrong side of the waistband. Press a skinny hem under the thin ends of the waistband.

With the right sides together, pin one long edge of the waistband to the pleated waist of the skirt. Have another check to see if the pleats look nice. If you're happy, go ahead and sew.

Press a skinny hem under the other long waistband edge.

Fold the waistband over and then hand-sew this just-pressed long edge to the inside of the skirt. Press again so everything looks hunky dory.

Put the zip in.

Try the skirt on and decide on the length. Cut with confidence.

Press a skinny hem on the bottom edge of the skirt. Press under a further 1cm and then sew. Join a campanology society to show off your new bell-shaped skirt.

A FLOUNCY SKIRT

I like a skirt that has volume, one that you can flounce around in, with a generous swish of fabric at the knees. You can make this skirt from different coloured strips of fabric, for a Zoom ice lolly look, or in different patterns so that you look like you are an inhabitant of planet patchwork, or use the same fabric for a more restrained flounce.

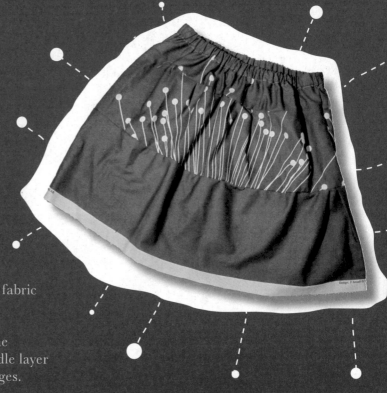

YOU'LL NEED:
160CM X 25CM *for the bottom layer*
140 CM X 20CM *for the middle*
120CM X 15CM *for the waistband*
ENOUGH WIDE ELASTIC *for the waistband, plus another* 3CM
PINS
IRON
2 SAFETY PINS
NEEDLE & THREAD

Zigzag the edges of all the pieces of fabric to stop them from fraying.

With the right sides together, pin the bottom layer of the skirt to the middle layer of the skirt along one of the long edges. Sew and press.

146

With the right sides together, pin that combined skirt layer to the top skirt layer along one of the long edges. Sew and press.

With the right sides together, sew the side seam.

Now for the waistband. Your skirt should be inside out.

Fold the waistband under 6mm and press.

Fold it over again. 2.5cm this time. Press.

This fold is going to be the casing for the elastic. So sew along the lower edge of that casing, but leave A GAP, so you can thread the elastic through.

Put the elastic around your waist. Note that measurement and then add another 2.5cm. Cut the elastic to that length.

Thread the elastic through the gap in the casing. I fastened safety pins to each end of the elastic, one I pinned to the waistband to stop the elastic getting lost in the casing, the other was a handy pulling tool for feeding the elastic through.

When it's all the way through, overlap the ends of the elastic, and safety pin them together.

Try on the skirt and make sure the elastic is comfy. Whip the skirt off if all is fine and dandy; if not, loosen or tighten the elastic.

Turn the skirt inside out and sew the overlapped ends of the elastic together. It might be a good idea to sew the overlapped ends a couple of times to make sure it's good and secure.

Hand-stitch the gap in the casing, and distribute the gathers evenly along the waistband.

If you fancy adding an extra bit of flounciness, you could gather 340cm x 7cm of fabric and sew it to the bottom of the skirt. Make the strip by sewing smaller pieces of fabric together. To gather it by hand, sew two parallel rows of running stitch along the long edge of the strip, leaving long tails of thread on either end of the strip.

Pull on these threads to gather the fabric. Then with the right sides together pin the gathered edge to the bottom pf the skirt. Sew.

By machine, adjust the stitch length – set it to longest length, and loosen the stitch tension, then sew two parallel rows of stitches along the top edge of the first piece of fabric.

And now for the hem. Press a skinny hem under the hem edge. Press a deeper hem under and then sew.

Sock Garters

with STARS, MOONS + A Sprinkling of tiny black BEADS

I had a moment of instant covetousness when I saw a pair of oatmeal catwalk cashmere socks decorated with golden pinwheels, and what looked like the workings of small expensive clocks. But then I begin to think practically: how would I wash them? This is my solution to the laundry dilemma.

YOU'LL NEED:
1 CARD *of* 1.5CM WIDE ELASTIC
THREAD
A HANDFUL *of* SILVER MOONS AND STARS,
    *with small holes, from the haberdashery
    department*
A *sprinkling of* TINY BLACK BEADS *from
    an old broken necklace*
TAPE MEASURE
NEEDLE

Measure your leg just below the knee, where the turn-over of your sock will nestle.

Cut a piece of elastic that's a couple of centimetres bigger than that measurement.

Overlap the edges of the elastic by 2cm and securely sew it with the needle and thread. The elastic should now be in a circle.

Assemble your beads, stars and moons in a little dish or saucer. Don't be tempted to heap them on the settee next to you – all the lovely shiny things will disappear behind the cushions.

148

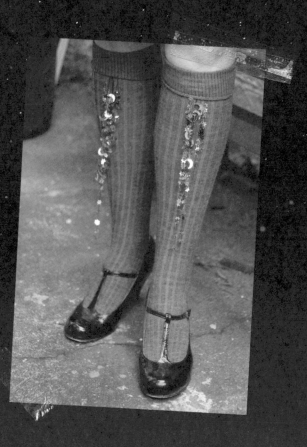

Thread on another star, and do exactly the same, just under the last star.

Add on a bead when you feel like it.

Add a moon.

Keep going until you're fairly nearly the end of the thread. Tie a knot in the end of the thread to prevent falling stars.

Attach another dangling thread next to the first one. Add stars, moons and beads. Tie a knot in the thread when you get to the end. Do this with another six or seven threads.

Snip a long dangly length of thread to sew a cascade of stars onto. The thread should reach from your sock turn-over to about mid shin.

Sew the thread to the inside of the circle of elastic, on the opposite side to the overlap.

One by one, thread the beads onto the thread, using the needle. Put the needle through the middle of the star, and bring it up to the top of the thread. Sew into the middle of the star a few times to keep it in its place.

Cut another piece of elastic, sew it into a circle and repeat.

Put on a pair of grey knee-length wool socks.

Pull the garters up, hide the elastic under the turn over of the sock. Look down and admire your starry legs.

And when you take your garters off for the evening, keep them as apart as star-crossed lovers. They have a habit of getting entangled.

POM-POM garters

Once you've learnt how, you can make garters with just about anything, from small gold safety pins and tiny gold moons bought at the haberdashery department, to small cogs stolen from your brother's bike, or, like here, with six lengths of brightly coloured wool and eight small pom-poms in lovely colours made by your own fair hands.

YOU'LL NEED:
6 LENGTHS *of* BRIGHTLY COLOURED WOOL
8 SMALL POM-POMS
1 CARD *of* 1.5CM WIDE ELASTIC
THREAD
TAPE MEASURE
NEEDLE

Make a garter with the elastic.

Plait three strands of the bright wool together. Sew four pom-poms on the plait like seed balls on autumn plane trees.

Sew the pom-pom-bedecked plait onto the elastic.

Make another garter to match.

A Pom-Pom NECKLACE

There's nothing nicer than a garland of pom-poms. And it also keeps your neck warm.

YOU'LL NEED:
A *lot of* POM-POMS *in a variety of colours and sizes*
CHUNKY WOOL *to thread the pom-poms onto*
1 STRIP *of* VELVET RIBBON, 50CM LONG *and about* 2CM *wide*
A TAPESTRY NEEDLE
NEEDLE & THREAD

Cut a long bit of chunky wool, there's no knowing how extravagant you might want your necklace to be once you get started.

Thread the tapestry needle with the chunky wool and then embark on this bloodthirsty instruction: stick the tapestry needle through the heart of the pom-pom and pull it onto the wool. Writing that made me think of Oscar Wilde's story: *The Nightingale and the Rose.* Luckily, we are only dealing with pom-poms here and not thorns, birds and unrequited love.

When you've threaded a fair few pom-poms on, drape them around your neck and see what you think. You can keep going and going and going, and abandon the idea of curtailing the pom-pom threading in favour of making a scarf.

Or you can STOP, and shimmy the pom-poms along the wool, until they are nicely bunched together, and there's a dangling bit of wool at either end of the pom-pom parade.

Double the wool over. Snip the velvet ribbon in half, and sew one tie to each end of the double-over wool. Tie the velvet ties in a jaunty bow, and wear your pom-poms with pride.

151

An ORNAMENTAL COLLAR

At a vintage fair recently, I spotted little detachable collars that had been decorated with thousands of beads. They were designed to brighten up a plain dress, and they were beautiful. I knew I'd never have enough patience to do the beadwork, but sequins and safety-pins are just as pleasing.

You'll need:
1 piece of boiled *or* felted wool, about 70cm x 15cm
A big box of safety pins
100cm of ribbon *to use as ties*
Paper
Felt pen
Tailor's chalk
Needle & thread

Decide on the shape of your collar. A big curve, a small curve, or a more odd shape entirely. Make a paper pattern to reflect the shape you've chosen, you could use the collar of a jacket as a template. Try the paper collar on, and see what you think. If you like it, hurray; if not, do a bit more newspaper snipping.

Fold the felted wool in half. Fold your pattern piece in half. Put the pattern piece on the fold of the fabric, and draw around it with the tailor's chalk.

Cut out carefully. Brush away the tailor's chalk.

Now for some lovely decoration. I sewed my safety pins into star shapes with the needle and thread, but you could scatter them any which way you like, or in regimented rows for a hint of military chic.

Cut the ribbon in half. Sew the ties to the collar.

152

A smaller ORNAMENTAL COLLAR

Make a paper pattern for the collar by drawing it on the paper with the felt pen (see picture).

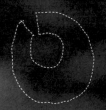

This collar is designed to be fastened snugly at the neck with a hook and eye, so bear that in mind when you draw the paper pattern.

YOU'LL NEED:
1 *piece of* BOILED *or* FELTED WOOL, *about* 30CM X 10CM
SEQUINS *in various colours*
1 HOOK & EYE
PAPER
FELT PEN
TAILOR'S CHALK
NEEDLE & THREAD

Fold the felted wool in half. Place the folded paper pattern piece on the fold of the fabric, and draw around it with the tailors chalk.

Cut out carefully. Brush away the tailor's chalk.

With the needle and thread, sew on the brightly coloured sequins. I left the bottom half of the collar undecorated for a nice contrast of grey wool and glitter.

Sew the hook on the neck edge of one side of the collar.

Sew the eye in a corresponding position on the opposite neck edge.

You can use big or small sequins and, for an additional touch of DIY glamour, sew a fringe of safety pins along the bottom of the collar. If you are going to go for safety-pin fringing, sew them on after the sequins, otherwise the thread keeps getting entangled in the pins.

An ODD-SHAPED COLLAR

This collar looks a bit like giant flattened ear muffs.

YOU'LL NEED:
1 PIECE *of* FELTED *or* BOILED WOOL,
   50CM X 50CM
A *lot of* BIG SEQUINS
100CM OF RIBBON *to use as ties*
TAILOR'S CHALK
NEEDLE AND THREAD

Draw this sort of shape on the newspaper with the felt pen.

Cut it out and drape it around your neck. Snip away until you are happy with the look.

Place the pattern piece onto the fabric.

Draw around it with the tailor's chalk. Cut out the odd-shaped collar from the boiled wool, or felted wool.

Sew overlapping rows of the big sequins onto the collar.

Cut the ribbon in half. Sew a tie to each neck edge of the collar.

A SCRIBBLE COLLAR

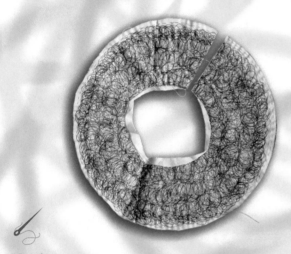

YOU'LL NEED:

AN OLD, SHINY, LARGE TABLE NAPKIN

1 PIECE *of* BOILED *or* FELTED WOOL *to use as a backing for the* SCRIBBLE COLLAR, *or another* TABLE NAPKIN

EMBROIDERY THREAD

100CM OF RIBBON *to use as ties*

EMBROIDERY NEEDLE

BIROS *in a variety of colours*

PAPER

FELT PEN

LP RECORD

PINS *(or safety pins)*

NEEDLE & THREAD

Draw around the LP with the felt pen onto the newspaper. Cut out the circle, then fold it in half and then in half again. Cut away a curve from the pointed corner. Undo the folded newspaper, and cut from the outside to the inside of the circle, so that the newspaper is in a collar shape. Try it on, and if you like it, head to the napkin.

Pin the paper pattern to the napkin. Cut out the collar shape. Cut the same shape out of the boiled wool, or the other table napkin.

With the vari-coloured Biros scribble all over the napkin collar.

With the embroidery thread and needle and some haphazard stitches, sew the scribbled napkin to the boiled wool or the other table napkin. Or you ditch the stitches and form an attachment with safety pins.

Cut the ribbon in half and sew a tie to each neck edge of the collar

Or you could fasten the collar with a BIG button. Choose the buttonhole stitch on your machine's stitch selector, and swap the everyday foot for the buttonhole one.

BELLBOY Hat

Even if you can't whistle a cheery tune and wink with a cheeky insouciance, you can still star in your own hotel comedy.

YOU'LL NEED:
1 PIECE *of* FELTED *or* BOILED WOOL, 50CM X 70CM
MEDIUM *to* HEAVY FUSIBLE INTERFACING, *about* 60CM X 25CM
1 STRIP *of* BIAS BINDING, *about* 60CM
1 STRIP *of* THIN ELASTIC, *about* 50CM
CEREAL BOWL
RULER
TAILOR'S CHALK
PINS
IRON
NEEDLE & THREAD

Draw around the cereal bowl with the tailor's chalk. I have quite a small head so I trimmed the circle a bit, until the diameter was about 18cm.

CROWN x 1

SIDE PANEL x 1

With the ruler, draw 1 rectangle 60cm x 9cm, if you're making a hat the same size as mine. If you're making it bigger, add extra centimetres to the length.

Cut out the shapes. You should have one circle, and one strip 60cm x 9cm.

Cut one circle of interfacing, and a strip 60cm x 9cm.

Iron the interfacing onto the circle of felted or boiled wool.

Iron the interfacing strip to the strip of felted or boiled wool.

With the right sides together, fold the interfaced strip in half widthways. Sew the 9cm edges.

With the right sides together, pin this to the interfaced circle. Sew. And then clip the curved seam, taking care not to cut through your neat little stitches.

Turn the hat the right way out.

Sew the bias binding along the hat's edge.

Perch the hat at a jaunty angle on your head and work out how much elastic you'll need. Cut the elastic, and sew it with neat little hand stitches to the inside of the hat. The elastic can nestle under your chin, or around the back of your head.

A Flowered Capelet

Instead of sauntering in a sweater, why not caper in a capelet. They are easy to make, and dashing to wear.

YOU'LL NEED:
1 PIECE *of* FELTED *or* BOILED WOOL *or* POLAR FLEECE, AS THESE WON'T FRAY, 50CM X 150CM
1 PIECE OF LINING, 50CM X 150CM
SCRAPS OF LEFTOVER FELTED WOOL *to make flowers*
A POPPER *or a* SAFETY PIN *to fasten the capelet*
NEWSPAPER
A FELT PEN
PINS
SCISSORS
IRON
NEEDLE & THREAD

Draw these two shapes onto newspaper, cut them out and pin them to the fabric like this:

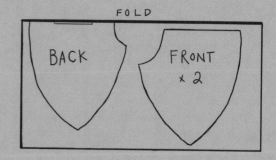

Cut them out carefully.

Pin the newspaper pattern pieces to the lining, in the same way as above, and cut those out carefully too.

Stay-stitch the front and back neck edges of the felted wool, about 1cm from the cut edge, to prevent the fabric edge from curling up like an old sandwich.

With the right sides together, sew the shoulder seams.

Notch the seams, and then press open so that they lie nice and flat.

If your lining is fine, thin cotton, say, zigzag the edges to stop them unravelling.

With the right sides together, sew the shoulder seams. Press.

Now for a flowery interlude. Cut out about 25 petal shapes.

Take your first petal and gently fold the petal end in half, and then hand sew it so that it doesn't unfurl. Do this with every petal in the pile.

Then sew the singular petals into trinities, by hand-sewing through the folded base of each flower.

Next with tiny, little stitches, almost invisible to the eye if you can manage it, sew all the trinities together in a cascading line. Admire your handiwork, and put it to one side for the moment.

With the right sides together, sew the lining to the cape, along the side edges and the neck, but not along the bottom edge.

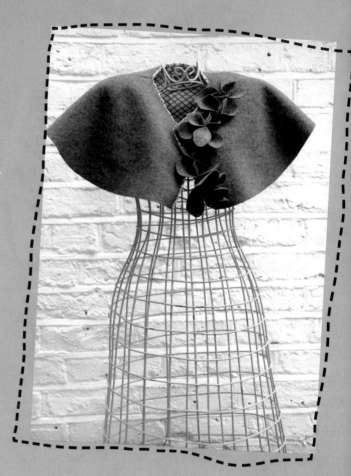

Flip the cape the right way round, and
then turn a tiny hem so that the bottom
of the lining isn't fluttering over the
bottom of the cape.

Now to add the cascade of felt flowers.
A little warning: make sure you only sew
the flowers to the felted bit of the cape and
not through the lining as well. I have a hasty
history, where shortcuts have ended up in a
long session with the seam ripper, and you
can probably guess the mistake I made, whilst
making this.So I put the cape across my knee,
with the felt bit on one side of my leg and
the lining flaring out over the other side to
prevent a further occurrence.

Pin the flowers to the cape, starting at the
neck, and draping them along one of the sides.

With the needle and thread, sew a few teensy
stitches through one of the topper-most petals
and the fabric of the cape. Move onto the next
cluster of three, and sew through one of these
petals and the fabric of the cape. Do this until
your flower cascade is securely sewn to the felt
cape. Stand up and hope that you haven't sewn
the cape to your skirt.

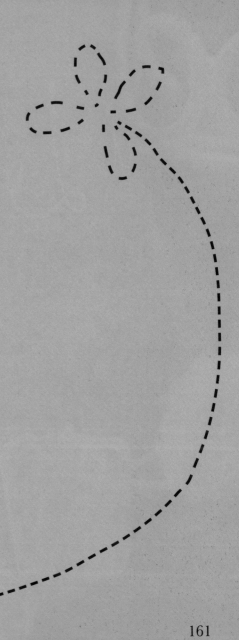

A Longer Capelet

You'll need:

1 piece *of* felted wool *or* polar fleece, 100cm x 150cm

1 strip *of* bias binding, 50cm

Light weight fusible interfacing *for the collar*, 60cm

1 toggle and loop *(or a small pom-pom and loop)*

Bigger pom-poms *for decorative purposes*

Newspaper

Felt pen

Scissors

Pins

Iron

Needle & thread

Draw the three pattern pieces onto the newspaper: one for the collar, one for the back and one for the sides.

Fold the fabric in half and pin the pattern pieces to the fabric like this:

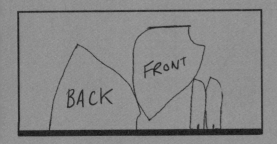

Cut them out. You should have two collar pieces, two side pieces, and one piece for the back. Because this fabric doesn't fray, you can ditch the zigzagging this time around.

Stay-stitch the neck edges of the cape.

With the right sides together sew the shoulder seams, notch them, and then press the seams open. If you do this really carefully, you could wear the cape inside out; the notched seams look like a decorative flourish, or the armoured plates of the stegosaurus.

Iron the interfacing to the wrong side of one of the collar pieces.

With the right sides together pin the collar along the little side edges and along the top, don't pin the bottom edges. Sew. Clip the seam and press. Turn the collar the right way out.

With the right sides together, pin one of the unsewn collar edges to the cape neck. Sew.

Flip the collar over, and hand sew the other edge of the collar to the inside of the cape neck.

Neatly sew the bias binding over those stitches, for a pretty finish.

On the front of the cape, sew a toggle and a loop to the neck as a cape fastener. Or a pom-pom and a loop. Add a few irresistible decorative pom-poms or two.

163

A Simple Silk Dress

I've had this fabric for ages; I bought it because I loved the colours and the feel of the tissue-fine silk. I then folded it away, unsure of what to make with it. But it was far too pretty to leave unused, so I decided on something simple and unstructured. I like the way it hangs, just so.

Fold one piece of the bodice fabric in half and then cut diagonally across one corner from 15cm in to 15cm down – this will be the neck.

Open the fabric out, place on top of the other piece of bodice fabric and, with the right sides together, sew along the shoulder seams.

With the right sides together, pin the two skirt pieces of the dress to the middle of the bodice. Make sure that it's perfectly balanced; otherwise you'll have one sleeve that's longer than the other.

Pin the sleeves, right sides together.

Sew along one sleeve and down one side.

Repeat with the other sleeve and side.

Hand-sew the satin or silk bias binding onto the 'V' of the bodice, and to the end of the sleeves.

You'll need:

1 piece of silk or fine cotton, 120cm x 150cm

Silk thread if you're using silk

A card of satin or silk bias binding, in a matching colour

A machine needle for the sewing of the silk material

Pins

Needle & thread

For the skirt bit of the dress, cut two rectangles of fabric, 50cm x 70cm.

For the bodice bit of the dress, cut two pieces of fabric 30cm x 115cm.

What if your damp hair miraculously froze into icicle strands... and every time you moved your head the strands clinked and chimed?

Outside when the trees are stark and bare, and the clouds are low, and have a hopeful affinity with snow, I am always inclined to ignore one bit of wintry weather advice: Don't go out with your hair wet, you'll get bad earache. Which is probably true, but what if instead of earache your damp hair miraculously froze into icicle strands, and every time you moved your head the strands clinked and chimed?

To counteract the earache potential, there are earmuffs and a detachable hood in pale sunshine yellow, and a scarf to match, with a scattering of brighter yellow pompoms, like the memory of crocus from spring, to be worn. And even if my hair refuses to freeze over, I can stand at the edge of the frozen lake in the park and skeeter stones across the white surface and listen to that strange eerie echo. If I was feeling vengeful and Gothic, I would also wear eerie clothes – a blackbird dress with a gold beak of a brooch, like the tatterdemalion wife of Dorian Gray's best friend 'whose dresses always looked as if they had been designed in a rage and put on in a tempest'. One year that will be my Christmas party outfit, inspired by Wilde's Lady Victoria, and the heroines of disaster movies who always end up with a cocktail dress in distress. But this year I will be leaning towards glitter-ball earrings, a net wrap decorated with a flurry of velvet ribbon and a skirt to take to the dance floor in.

Because I am more giddy than Gothic, in the daytime I will take my sartorial cues from an absconding Russian Sixties spy in a shag-pile hat and reversible mittens made from a recycled tee and a scrappy bit of fun fur, and a poncho, but not the sort that Clint Eastwood would wear.

And I will savour my favourite thing about winter – which is how you bring the cold in with you from the outside. For moments, the freezing weather is in the room with you, nestled against the wool of a huge crocheted scarf, until the indoor heat warms up everything, and all the lovely chilliness disappears. Then you can shrug off some of the layers and settle down to a bit of tipsy patchworking, and pilfering the letters from the Scrabble board to turn into jewellery. More wintry advice: practise ignoring irate expressions, handy for when your cohorts realise you have transformed the Z into an earring.

Xmas decoration Earrings

One breath-in-the-air winter's day, when I was wandering over Albert Bridge, I saw two people disguised as Christmas Trees, swigging from a sliver hip flask. They were covered all over with springy Scotch pines boughs, bedecked with tinsel and baubles, and with big starry hats on their heads, and they were wandering nonchalantly into town, as if they dressed like that every day. These earrings are homage to their Yuletide spirit, and the instructions are so easy that I am almost too embarrassed to scribble them down.

YOU'LL NEED:
CHRISTMAS BAUBLES *(I used mini glitterballs from the supermarket)*
EARRING FIXTURES
PLIERS

Open the little loop on the earring fixture with the pliers.

Hang the loop of your chosen bauble onto the open loop of the earring fixture.

Close the loop on the earring fixture with the pliers. Put the earrings on your ears. Um, that's it.

And because they are so simple you could make a whole host of winter wonderland ear accessories. Pretty petal shaped buttons in pale colours would look like frosted flowers, and clear, glass ones like the tiny droplets of sparkling frozen water that collect on bare branches on the coldest of mornings.

In fact, don't stop there. Scupper any marathon Scrabble games by stealing the letters and making them into wordy earrings and rings. You'll need pliers and some bits and bobs from the craft shop. Buy ring backs and earring settings, jump rings and some glue.

Simply glue the Scrabble tile to the ring back, and to make the earrings, pierce holes in the top of the tiles… and with pliers open the jump rings and thread one through the hole in the tile. You can attach it straight to the earring, but if you want a more dangly effect, make a little chain of interlocking jump rings, and then apply the pliers to the earring. And you don't have to stick to one tile either, spell out your favourite word with a tidy column of tiles, by piercing holes in the top and bottom of the tiles and connecting them with jump rings. Use the same skill sets, and some strong glue, to transform Monopoly or Cluedo pieces – there's no need to be bored of board games after you've liberated the pieces for decorative motives.

Or make a ring out of blown fuses. All you need is a ring back (John Lewis sell them in packs of three and they cost a couple of pounds), strong glue and three old fuses. Glue the fuses together, then glue them to the ring back and leave to dry. And then make a matching circuitboard necklace, by threading ribbon through the circuit holes in the top and tying in a bow around your neck.

If this all sounds a little prosaic, and you're looking for inspiration of a more fantastical nature I'd recommend the avant-garde artist Elsa Von Freytag-Loringhoven, known as the mama of Dada, who had very unexpected accessories. She painted her shaved-head scarlet, wore a birthday cake with lit candles as a hat, and a birdcage around her neck, populated with chirping canaries. She favoured emerald-green cheeks instead of pale-pink blusher, used gilded porcupine quills as false eyelashes and postage stamps as beauty spots, and transformed ice-cream spoons into earrings.

AN EVENING BAG
with BANGLES for HANDLES

In Claire Wilcox's *Bags* (V&A Publications), she describes a scene from Lord Melville's impeachment trial in 1806, which was graced by 'rows of pretty peeresses, who sat eating sandwiches from silk indispensables'. Indispensables were small bags, usually filled to the brim with the essential objects of daily life – rouge, fan, handkerchief, smelling salts, love letters. This evening bag – which has mismatched bangles for handles – is perfect for storing your lipstick and door keys on a night out, or a cheese roll for an engrossing day at the Old Bailey.

YOU'LL NEED:

2 BANGLES, *they don't need to match, in fact, it's almost nicer if they don't*

1 PIECE OF FABRIC, 24CM X 48CM

1 PIECE OF FABRIC, 24CM X 48CM, *for the lining*

SEQUINS

POM-POMS *(optional)*

1 GLITTERBALL *(optional)*

NEEDLE & THREAD

IRON

Fold the fabric in half, widthways, and then in half again, lengthways. From the unfolded corner, put a pin 14cm down from the top edge. Put another pin 7cm in along the top edge. Then cut a diagonal slant from pin to pin. Round off the edges at both ends of the first piece of fabric. This sounds complicated, but it really isn't! You should have this sort of shape:

Do the same with the lining piece of fabric. Unfold both pieces of fabric and press nice and flat.

Zigzag the edges of both pieces of fabric.

Fold the lining in half, widthways, right sides together, and sew the side seams

Fold the outer piece of fabric in half, widthways, right sides together, and sew the side seams.

Turn the outer piece of fabric the right way out. Leave the lining inside out. Pop the outer piece of fabric into the lining.

Bear in mind, before you start the next sewing steps, that this is a bag that you want to pop a small bottle of perfume into and a Russian red lipstick, so don't sew up the top edge.

Now, sew the lining and the outer fabric together – sew along the first slanted edge, keep going along the rounded edge, head down the next slanted side seam. Keep going up the next slanted side seam, around the rounded end, and then STOP. You should have one unsewn slanted side seam.

Clip the corners, neatly, but don't cut through the freshly sewn stitches.

Trim the seams with equal care.

Pull the bag through the unsewn slanted side seam.

Turn in the edges of the side seam. Press neatly, and then hand-sew so that the zigzagged edges are hidden.

Grab one of the bangles, and place it on the outside of the bag, near the top of the rounded edge. Fold over the rounded edge, so that the bangle forms a handle, and there's a little bit of the lining prettily overlapping the outside fabric. Pin, and then hand-sew – it's easier than trying to negotiate the fabric and bangle combo under the machine needle.

Do the same thing with the other bangle.

Hand-sew on two small pom-poms and one bigger mirrored disco ball.

You can change the dimensions of the bag, and, if you use fabric with a distinctive, bold print, you could cut a tumble of motifs and make a dangling decoration to adorn your evening bag. I cut out lots of leaves from a piece of vivid cotton, hand-sewed them back to back and then hand-sewed the leaves to a couple of very skinny bits of fabric, like leaves on a branch. Then I sewed the fabric twigs and leaves to the top of the bag.

If you've made the bag using a plainer fabric, a rough-and-ready tasselled ornament, made from left-over strips of fabric, looks effective, too. Bundle some skinny strips of fabric together, then tie them around the middle with another skinny fabric strip. Hand-sew to the evening bag.

PRETTY Bow FOR YOUR HAIR

It's easy to make lovely little bows, bigger bows and HUGE bows to decorate your lovely locks. For small bows, unravel a few rolls of thin ribbon, grab some hairgrips, cheap plastic hairbands and some glue. Make a cup of tea, put on a Busby Berkely musical – I'd *YouTube* the beautiful 'By A Waterfall', from *Footlight Parade*, and get sticking and sewing.

LITTLE BOWS

YOU'LL NEED:
HAIRGRIPS *or* CHIGNON PINS
300CM *of* SKINNY RIBBON
*in French revolutionary
colours (Maybe with
the addition of some
Schiaparelli Pink)*
GLUE GUN

Snip the ribbon into 30cm lengths.

Tie neat little bows.

Glue them onto the hair grips.

Wait for the glue to dry completely
before adding to your beehive.

BIGGER BOWS

YOU'LL NEED:
GIANT HAIR CLIPS, *or* **A STIFF HAIRBAND**
1 PIECE *of* FABRIC, 18CM X 20CM
1 PIECE *of* FABRIC, 12CM X 10CM
1 PIECE *of* FABRIC, 10CM X 3CM
NEEDLE & THREAD
IRON
GLUE

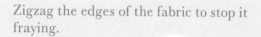

Zigzag the edges of the fabric to stop it fraying.

With the right sides together, fold the fabric in half, lengthways, and sew the sides, then the long seam, but leave a GAP, so that you can turn your potential bow the right way out.

Clip the corners, being careful not to snip your stitches.

Turn the bow the right way out. Hand-sew the gap.

Roughly pleat the middle of the rectangle into a nice bow shape, and hand-sew the middle of the pleats. You can wind the thread around the middle after you've finished stitching, for an extra bit of bow security.

Do exactly the same with the smaller piece of fabric.

Sew the little bow to the big bow.

Zigzag the edges of the smallest piece of fabric. Press a skinny hem under on all sides.

Wrap the nicely pressed little strip around the middle of the sewn-together bows. Sew the strip at the back.

With a generous blob of glue, stick the bows to the giant hairclip, or to the stiff hairband.

Make sure the glue is **DRY** before you try them on.

Large Bows

You'll Need:
Metal hair snaps *or* alligator clips *(as the name suggests, they are the ones with teeth)*
300cm *of* wider ribbon, *about* 4cm *wide*
50cm *of* thinner ribbon, *about* 3cm *wide*
Needle
Thread
Glue

Cut half of the wider ribbon into 22cm strips, and cut the other half of the ribbon into 12cm strips.

With the right sides together, zigzag each strip of ribbon into a loop.

Turn the ribbon loops the right way round. With the zigzag seam at the back, pinch the centre of the ribbon so that the ribbon becomes bow-shaped. With the needle and thread sew securely across the centre of the ribbon to maintain that bow shape.

Sew a smaller bow to the middle of a bigger bow. Sew a little bit of the thin ribbon around the middle of both bows.

Glue the double bow to the ends of the metal hair snaps.

179

GIANT BOWS

You'll need:
1 piece *of* fabric, 80cm x 12cm
1 piece *of* fabric, 12cm x 8cm
1 big hair slide (*or a hairband*)
Glue
Needle & thread

Zigzag the edges.

Fold the fabric in half, widthways.

With the right sides together, sew along the two long edges; don't sew the small edge.

Turn the strip the right way out.

Hand-sew the small open end.

Sew the little ends together. You should now have a loop of fabric.

Press the loop, so that your just-sewn seam is centred at the back.

Scrunch the fabric into a bow shape and sew.

With the smaller piece of fabric, zigzag the edges.

With the right sides together, sew around two of the edges.

Turn the fabric the right way out, and hand-sew the gap closed. Sew the strip around the middle of your giant bow. Then glue or sew to the hair clip, or the hair band.

Wear them proudly in your hair and practise sweeping bows like Buttons in *Cinderella*, in your pretty bows.

more RiBBON fun

After the French Revolution, aristos who survived the chop had parties to celebrate – the legendary *bals des victimes*. The men bowed their heads as if they were about to be guillotined. The ladies adopted the coiffure *à la victime*, and wore shift dresses decorated with red lace. Others wore thin red ribbons around their necks – a macabre nod to the cut of the blade.

A Saved from the Guillotine Choker

YOU'LL NEED:
100CM *of* RED VELVET RIBBON, 2CM
RED BEADS
BEADING NEEDLE
THREAD

Cut enough red velvet ribbon to tie around
your neck with a bow at the back.

Thread a few red beads onto the thread,
and sew to the back of the bottom of the
ribbon. Thread more red beads onto more
thread, and sew to the ribbon, so that it
looks like a beaded fringe.

Tie in a neat bow around your unsevered neck.

In the incredibly beautiful, incredibly long
Stanley Kubrick film of Thackeray's *Barry
Lyndon*, actress Gay Hamilton wore a ribbon
choker around her neck. Having blindfolded
Ryan O'Neill, she says: 'I have taken the ribbon
from around my neck and hidden it somewhere
on my person. You are free to look for it
wherever you like, and I should think very little
of you if you do not find it.' She had placed it
down the front of her bodice. Oh la la.

183

A TULLE WRAP

with velvet bows

Decorated with a flurry of velvet bows, this wraps looks romantically old fashioned.

YOU'LL NEED:

200CM *of* TULLE *or* NET. *Tulle is soft and dearer. Net is cheaper, but a little scratchy*

22CM OF THIN VELVET RIBBON *for each bow*

24CM-26CM OF WIDER VELVET RIBBON FOR LARGER BOWS *(I bought about 20m of ribbon)*

NEEDLE & THREAD

Tie the cut ribbon in bow shapes, and make a big, velvety pile of them.

Fold the net in half, lengthways.

Hand-sew the velvet bows to the tulle or net. You can sew through both layers of the net, or just on the top layer. Either way looks lovely.

A Skirt to go dancing in

I love dancing. In my dreams,
I would join a dance troupe like
The Actionettes, and do routines
dressed as an airhostess or a
Mexican wrestler. Until the magical
day arrives, I'll content myself with
a disco mix tape and this skirt.
It has a slightly swingy shape, lies
just below your waistline and is
perfect for twisting the night away.

YOU'LL NEED:
1 PIECE *of* FABRIC, 150CM X 150CM
18CM ZIP
60CM *of* LIGHTWEIGHT FUSIBLE INTERFACING
HOOK *and* EYE
2 CARDS *of* BIAS BINDING
NEWSPAPER
FELT PEN
SCISSORS
PINS
IRON
ZIPPER FOOT
NEEDLE
THREAD

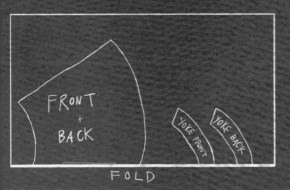

Draw the pattern pieces onto a newspaper with a felt tip. Cut them out with paper scissors.

Fold the fabric in half, pin the pattern pieces to the fabric, and then cut around them. You should have a skirt front and a skirt back, and two pieces for the front waistband, and two pieces for the waistband's back.

Cut the interfacing for the waistband, a piece for the front, a piece for the back.

Zigzag all the edges of the fabric to stop them from fraying.

Stay-stitch the top edge on the front piece of the skirt. Do the same with the top edge on the back piece of the skirt.

Press the interfacing to one front waistband piece, and one waistband back piece.

With the right sides together, sew the side seam of these two waistband pieces – you should now have a long strip of fabric made up of a front waistband piece and a back waistband piece. Press that little seam.

With the right sides together, sew the other front waistband piece to the other back waistband piece. Press that little seam. Leave this to one side for the moment.

Now with the right sides together, pin one of the side seams of the skirt.

With the right sides together, pin the interfaced waistband to the top of the skirt, making sure that both side seams are aligned.

Sew the side seam, all the way from the hem of the skirt to the top of the waistband.

Press the side seam.

Grab hold of the waistband piece that you left aside. With the right sides together, pin it to the top edge of the interfaced waistband, which is already attached to the skirt. Sew and then press.

Press a little seam to the wrong side of the end of the waistband.

Press a little hem to the wrong side all the way along the newly attached waistband.

Flip that waistband over and hand-sew the waistband to the inside of the skirt with small, neat stitches.

With the right sides of the skirt together, sew the other side seam, but STOP 18 cm from the top, this is where your zip is going to take up residence.

Swap the ordinary foot for the zipper foot on the machine and put the zip in.

Hand-sew the hook and eye above the zip for neat closure.

Try on your skirt and work out how long or short you want the skirt to be. Cut it to the required length.

Zigzag those freshly snipped edges.

Hand-sew the bias binding along the skirt's hem.

Try the skirt on again and practise a few moves.

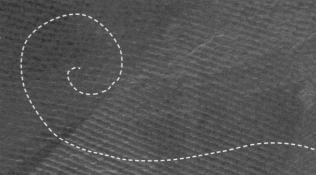

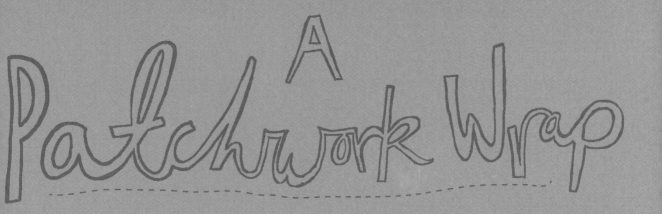

A Patchwork Wrap

There's something very old fashioned about sitting by the (gas) fire on a dark winter's evening with a pile of scrappy fabric on the floor, preparing yourself for a stint of patchworking, with a glass of seasonal sherry at your elbow. I am not courageous enough to attempt a quilt of the dimensions that would fit a four-poster bed but an evening wrap, with a long patchwork panel seemed achievable. The sherry provides a tipsy gravitas to the traditional proceedings.

YOU'LL NEED:

ENOUGH SCRAP FABRIC *to make a patchwork strip which measures* 188CM X 20CM. *I used squares that were* 11CM X 11CM, *and rectangles that were* 20CM X 9CM *There were* 32 SQUARES *and* 7 RECTANGLES

1 PIECE *of* FABRIC, 188CM X 100CM *(I used an old shiny bed spread)*

SEQUINS *and* BEADS *(optional)*

PENCIL

LOTS *of* PAPER *to make the templates (I used the free magazines that are popped through the letterbox)*

RULER

PAPER SCISSORS

TAILOR'S CHALK

NEEDLE

TWO DIFFERENT COLOURS *of* THREAD, *one in a contrasting colour to your patchwork theme, another that will blend in nicely*

PINS

Draw your two templates – an 11cm x 11cm square and a 20cm x 9cm rectangle - with the ruler, pencil and paper. Cut them out with the paper scissors, NOT your fabric scissors.

Place them on your patchwork fabric, draw around them with the tailor's chalk and then cut out 32 squares and 7 rectangles.

Now it's back to the paper, scissors, ruler and pencil. Draw 32 squares that measure 9cm x 9cm, and 7 rectangles that are 18cm x 7cm on the free magazine. These smaller squares and rectangles are going to be used as a temporary backing as you're sewing the pieces together by hand. (You could miss out the next few steps entirely and machine-stitch all the squares and rectangles as you go, then press all of the seams, but there is something very cosy about sewing these by hand, with Rosemary's Baby on in the background.)

Put your template on the wrong side of your patchwork fabric. Using the bold stand-out coloured thread, tack a 1cm hem around three sides of each square. Usually you would seam around all four sides but as the shiny fabric is going to be a border, you only need to tack three sides. On the rectangular pieces, tack a 1cm hem around the template on the two long sides.

Spread the patchwork pieces on the floor and move them around, like those little puzzles with the sliding squares, until you come up with an arrangement of colours and patterns that you like the look of.

Sew the squares and rectangles together in your chosen pattern. Make sure that you don't sew through the paper templates, as these are going to be whipped out sometime in the near future.

Finished sewing all the squares and rectangles together? You can now whip out the paper templates.

Now's the time to hand-sew the beads or sequins to the patchwork if you want your wrap to look even more fancy.

Next cut the big piece of fabric into one 60cm x 188cm piece and two 20cm x 88cm pieces.

Zigzag the edges of the wrap fabric to stop it fraying.

Pin the right sides of the two smaller pieces of wrap fabric to the right side of the patchwork strip, along its length, and machine-sew them together.

Pin the right side of this patchwork-plus-fabric strip to the right side of the large piece of fabric around three of the sides, leaving one width edge unpinned. Machine-stitch around the three pinned edges.

Press a hem to the wrong side of the
unsewn width edges.

Turn the wrap the right way out, and
neatly hand sew the width edge.

Wrap the wrap dramatically
around your shoulders,
and think of sparkling
drinks, parquet floors
and chandeliers.

A CRAZY PATCHWORK BAG

If squares and rectangles are a little too orderly, you could always head for the wildness of crazy patchwork. It probably started in hard-scrabble America, as a way of making economy quilts. Because it's stitched out of fabric that's different sizes and shapes, every last bit of cloth could be used, shirts, flannel vests, old dresses, bits of raggedy blankets. The Victorians, taking advantage of wealth and trade routes, were bonkers for it, stitching together far more lush and exotic fabrics; their crazy patchworks were symphonies in silk and satin, and velvets, with embroidery worked over the top, and braid and sequins added willy-nilly. It's easy to achieve your own moment of quaint glittery brilliance in the form of a patchwork bag.

LOTS *of* GLORIOUS SCRAPS OF FABRIC, *cut into
a medley of small shapes and sizes*
2 PIECES *of* FABRIC, 26CM X 14CM, *on which
to assemble the patchwork*
2 PIECES *of* THINNER BACKING FABRIC,
26CM X 14CM, *to hide all your messy stitches*
BEAD AND SEQUINS, BROKEN BITS *of*
NECKLACE *and* SMASHED SHINY BROOCHES
A 24CM ZIP
A LOOP *of* FABRIC
A D-RING
A BANGLE
NEEDLE & THREAD
PINS

Zigzag the edges of the fabric.

Pin the patchwork scraps to the two pieces of assembly fabric in a haphazardly pretty way.

Then zigzag around the edges of the scraps, which will not only anchor them to the fabric but also prevent the off-kilter patches from fraying too much.

Add on a bit of judicious beading, sequins and magpie treasure, by hand-sewing them in place. Leave a little gap around the edges, so that you don't break the sewing-machine needle with the trinketry when you come to sew the bag together.

Tack one piece of backing fabric to the back of the patchwork to hide the stitches. Do the same with the other piece.

With right sides together, tack the two pieces together along one of the long edges.

Fold it open, so that it looks like an open book.

Swap the ordinary machine foot for the zipper and sew the closed zip in the centre of the tacked seam.

OPEN up the zip, and then pin around the three sides, right side together.

Sew the three sides.

Carefully clip the corners.

Turn the bag the right way out, through the open zip.

Sew the fabric loop on one side of the bag.

Attach the D-ring to the fabric loop.

Attach the bangle to the D-ring.

Attach the bangle to your wrist, and let your wildly imaginative bag dangle and spin.

A Poncho that Clint Eastwood
probably wouldn't wear.

The word poncho conjures up many an image. For some people, it's Clint Eastwood, wrapped in a horse blanket and smoking a cheroot. Mine has more to do with girls in garage bands and go-go boots.

With the right sides together, sew * to **.
Press.

Sew + to ++. Press.

You'll need:
2 pieces *of* cosy fabric, 80cm x 40cm
   *(you could use an old blanket, thick fleece,
   chequered wool)*
2 pieces *of* cosy fabric, 80cm x 40cm,
   if you are going to line the poncho
2 cards *of* matching *or* contrasting bias
   binding, 250cm x 25mm *(if you're going
   to add lining, you won't need as much bias
   binding, one card of 250cm will do, as you'll
   only be sewing it around the neck)*
Pins
Iron

To add some shape, put a couple of darts in.
Turn the poncho inside out, place a pin on each
neck edge, where your shoulders are. Take the
poncho off. Don't scratch yourself.

Sew the darts, 8cm wide, 10cm deep. Press.

Hand-sew the bias binding around the bottom
edges of the poncho.

Hand-sew the bias binding around the neck
edges.

Zigzag the edges of the fabric to stop them
fraying.

Lay out the two pieces on the floor, right sides
up, like this:

For the lining, make the poncho in exactly the
same way, but don't sew on the bias binding yet.

With the right sides together, sew the poncho
and the lining along the bottom edges. Then
turn the poncho the right way out through the
open neck.

Sew the lining and the poncho together, very
near the neck edge, and then hand-sew the
bias binding around the neck for a pretty, neat
finish.

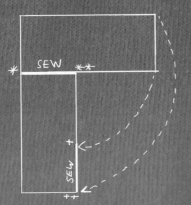

195

A PONCHO with a pocket
and some blanket stitch

196

YOU'LL NEED:

2 PIECES *of* COSY FABRIC, 80CM X 40CM
1 SQUARE PIECE *of* COSY FABRIC,
   27CM X 27CM, *to make the pocket*
1 CARD *of* BIAS BINDING *(or 6cm x 82cm strip*
   of knitting)
A FEW POM-POMS
BRIGHT KNITTING WOOL
PINS
IRON
TAPESTRY NEEDLE

Make up the poncho as above. (The darts are optional).

With the bright wool and the tapestry needle, blanket-stitch along the bottom edges of the poncho.

Zigzag the edges of the 27cm square piece of fabric.

Press a skinny hem under on all sides of the square. Sew.

Pin the square pocket to the front of the poncho, so that the square is like a diamond.

Sew along the two diamond sides that are nearest the bottom of the poncho. Don't sew the ones nearest the top, this is where your hands are going to be nestling when you're wearing the poncho.

Sew the top point of the diamond to the poncho. Sew over it a few times to make sure it's securely in place.

Sew the bias binding, or the strip of knitting, around the neck edge.

Add a few brightly coloured pom-poms to the neckline.

Put on your skating boots and a stocking cap and pretend you are in a winter wonderland photo by Jacques Henri Lartigue, the well-to-do French photographer who took snaps of his friends cavorting on ice rinks and ski runs.

A POM-POM SCARF

A pom-pom scarf to match your
warm poncho would be a fine thing

YOU'LL NEED:
1 PIECE *of* FABRIC, 115CM X 17CM
2 CARDS *of* MATCHING *or* CONTRASTING,
  BIAS BINDING, 25MM X 250CM
A pile of FLUFFY POM-POMS
NEEDLE & THREAD

Zigzag the edges of the strip of fabric.

Sew the bias binding around the edges.

Randomly sew the pom-poms to the scarf, at
either end, threading the needle through the
centre of each pom-pom.

A Hand-Warmer

YOU'LL NEED:
2 PIECES *of* FAKE FUR, 34CM X 50CM
110CM *of* RIBBON *or* CORD
PINS
NEEDLE
THREAD

Trim the edges of the fake fur to make it easier to sew.

Smooth the pile away from the edge, and with the right sides together, fold one piece of fake fur in half and pin along the long side, to make a tube.

Sew along the pinned seam.

Whip out the pins, and flatten the seam open with your hand. A hot iron and fake fur are not a good combination.

Do exactly the same as above with the second piece of fake fur.

Turn one of the tubes the right way out, leave the other inside out. Slide the right-way-out tube inside the inside-out tube – so the right sides are together.

Pin one of the short ends together, and machine stitch.

Pull the whole hand-warmer through the unsewn end. And then tuck the lining piece of fake fur so that it nestles inside the hand-warmer. Hand-sew the unsewn edge.

Pin one end of the ribbon or cord to each end of the hand-warmer, to make a big loop. Drape the loop around your neck, to check the position of the hand-warmer. Happy? Hand-sew the ribbon or cord in place.

Reversible Mittens

I like wearing mittens, they make me feel I have been temporarily transformed into a puppet. These ones are reversible, and made from fun fur and the sleeves of an old T-shirt. With a bit of practice, it'll take you about ten minutes to make a pair.

YOU'LL NEED:

4 PIECES *of* QUITE STRETCHY T-SHIRT FABRIC, APPROX 30CM X 20CM *(depending on your hand size)*

4 PIECES *of* FUN FUR, 30CM X20CM *(depending on your hand size)*

40CM *of* BRAID *(for an optional trim)*

PAPER

FELT PEN

PINS

Make the mitten pattern by drawing generously around your slightly spread-out hand on the paper. Add on an extra 5cm at the wrist for the turned-up cuff. Cut out the mitten shapes.

Zigzag the edges of the fabric.

Pin two of the T-shirt fabric pieces, right sides together, and then pin the mitten pattern to them, and carefully cut around it.

Do the same with two pieces of the fake fur.

Whip out the pins.

With the right side still together, lay the T-shirt mitten shapes directly on top of the fun fur mitten shapes. Pin to stop the layers slipping around.

Sew all four pieces together around the mitten shape, but not across the cuff.

Whip out the pins, and separate the top layer of the T-shirt fabric, and roll it up the body of the mitten, as if you were turning it inside out.

Poke the thumb through.
Now the T-shirt should cover
both sides of the glove.

Here's where you can make
the fur cuff. Turn the fur side
2cm over onto the T-shirt
fabric. Sew around the cuff,
by hand or on the machine,
the choice is yours.

Then carefully hand-sew
the braid around the top of
the cuff, with the tiniest of
stitches so that they don't
show tooooo much when you
reverse the mittens.

201

A Hood

A poncho is lovely and snuggly, as
is the pom-pom scarf, but to add to
the winter glow, consider the allure
of a hood, or a fake fur hat. Here
are both.

YOU'LL NEED:
PIECE *of* FELTED WOOL *or* FLEECE,
64CM X 48CM
PIECE *of* FUN FUR, 64CM X 48CM
STRIP *of* FELTED WOOL *or* FLEECE,
62CM X 12CM
CARD *of* WIDE BIAS BINDING *(optional)*
big SNAP FASTENERS
A HOODED SWEATSHIRT *to use as a pattern*
NEEDLE & THREAD
NEWSPAPER
PENCIL
FELT PEN
PAPER SCISSORS
PINS

Using the hood of your hoodie, make a paper pattern. Pop it flat onto the paper and draw around it with the pencil. Whip the hoodie out of the way and draw over the pencil marks with the felt pen to make it easier to see.

Cut out the paper pattern with the paper scissors.

Fold the felted wool in half. Pin the paper pattern to the wool. Cut out. You should now have two felted-wool hood pieces, which measure 32cm x 24 cm.

Zigzag the edges.

Pin the right sides of the wool together, along the crown, and down the back. Carefully try it on and see what you think. If it's like a sun visor over your forehead you might consider trimming it back a tad. If it seems a-okay, sew.

Now for the fake fur. As it has a pile, make sure that the furriness is all heading in the same direction. Fold the fake fur in half; it's easier to cut if the un-furry side is on the outside. Pin the paper pattern to the fake fur, and cut out the hoodie shapes. You should now have two fake fur hood pieces which measure 32cm x 24cm.

Fake fur can be tricky to sew. You're going to be sewing the right sides together, so crop the fur back along the edges on the crown and the back seam allowance, then pin those trimmed right sides together and sew.

It's also worth trimming the sides that surround your face too. But don't cut off too much.

Leave the fake fur hood inside out. Turn the wool hood the right way out. Pop the wool hood inside the fur hood; the right sides of the fabric should be together. Pin around the edges that will frame your face, and sew very close to the edges.

Turn the hood the right way out by pulling it through the unsewn neck edge. If you like, hand-sew bias binding around the edges of the hood that frame your face.

Hand-sew bias binding around the 62cm x 12cm strip of fabric.

Fold the strip in half, wrong sides together, lengthways, and press.

Drop the hood a little way in between the two edges of the wool strip; like making a sandwich, the hood is the filling, leave an extra strip of fabric on either side of the hood. Pin and machine-stitch.

Try on the hood, and overlap the extra strips of fabric to see where the snap fasteners should go. Pop pins in to remind you.

Hand-sew on the two big snap fasteners.

A fake fur HAT

In my head I imagine that I look like a spy, waiting at a Moscow rail station for an elusive contact to appear out of the freezing fog. On my head, this hat probably looks like a fake fur version of the liquorice allsorts that nobody ever eats.

YOU'LL NEED:
1 PIECE *of* FAKE FUR, 65CM X 54CM (*I've used the sort that looks a bit like a shag-pile rug; for a more chic creation you could use fake fur with a more compact pile and a sleeker colour*)
PINS
COMPASS
NEEDLE & THREAD

Cut two circles from the fabric. Their diameter should be approx 21cm.

CROWN
x 1

SIDE PANEL
X 2

Cut two strips, 65cm x 18cm, from the fake fur.

Trim the edges of the fur, to make it easier to sew.

With the right sides together, pin the side of one of the strips of fake fur to make a tube. Try it on to see if it fits. If it does, sew the right sides together.

With the right sides together, pin the fake fur tube to one of the circles.

Try on the makeshift hat and see what you think. If you're happy, get stitching.

Clip the seams. Notch the circular seam.

Repeat all of the steps above with the other fake-fur circle and fake-fur strip.

Turn one of the hats inside out, and leave the other the right way out. Pop the right-way-out hat inside the inside-out hat. Sew around the bottom edge, leaving a gap of about 6cm.

Carefully pull the whole hat through the gap, and hand-sew it closed.

Brush away the spores of fake fur that are layering every object in the room, imagining that it's snow blowing in from the Russian Steppes.

EAR MUFFS

Oh, the joy of warm ears in winter.
You can make these muffs compact
and cute or large and funny. Mine
are somewhere in the middle.

YOU'LL NEED:
1 STIFF HAIRBAND, *about* 3CM WIDE
1 PIECE *of* FAKE FUR, 75CM X 30CM
NEEDLE & THREAD
PEN
PAPER
PINS
BIG MUG (*or a compass*)
SCISSORS

Using the big mug as a template, draw a couple of circles onto the paper. Cut out the circles with paper scissors.

On the wrong side of the fake fur, pin the paper circles to the fabric, and cut out four circles. Clip the edges of the fake fur to make it easier to sew.

Cut a strip of fake fur, 35cm x 6cm. Clip the edges of the fake fur.

With the right sides together, pin two fur circles together, leaving an opening of 5cm at the top.

Machine stitch them together, but don't sew the 5cm gap.

Take out the pins and turn the circles the right way out.

Do the same with the other two circles.

Cut up some of the left-over fur and stuff it into the 5cm gaps so that your ear muff is nice and plump.

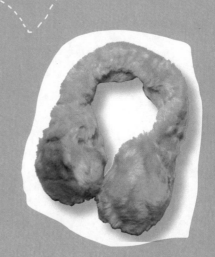

With the right sides together, and along the long edge, pin the fake fur strip. Sew along the pinned edge. Whip out the pins, and turn the tube the right way out.

Slide the tube onto the hairband.

Pop a fake fur circle onto the end of the hairband. Hand-sew the gap, and at the same time hand-sew the circle to the tube, to make it nice and secure. Pop the remaining circle onto the other end of the hairband, and hand-sew that securely, too.

Felted Wool

Now that the trees are bare and the evenings are long, it's time to retrieve the jumpers that you stored away in spring. Hopefully the lavender bags did their trick and your knitwear hasn't been turned to woolly lace by hungry moths.

But if they look bedraggled to your wintry weather eye, you could transform them into something else. The trick is to stop thinking of them as jumpers, and imagine them as a source of new fabric. Here's where felting comes in. You need a bundle of 100 per cent wool jumpers, cardies, or old blankets, a washing machine set to hot for the washing bit, and to cold for the rinse cycle. Add in washing powder and a clean towel or a pair of jeans. The hot water will change the structure of the wool – remember that disastrous day when you accidentally shrank your dad's cashmere jumper, and it came out small and matted when it had been sleek and large? Well, this is exactly the effect you want here.

The jeans or the towel help with the agitation, a vital part of the felting process.

When you take your changed woollies out of the machine, spread them out flat to dry. And then you can get snipping and sewing. You could make the reversible mittens (see page 200) with the felted wool, transform it into a bag, or a scarf, out of sewn-together panels of felted wool decorated with bright felted-wool circles.

Embellished Felted Leaves

Draw a few leaf shapes onto the paper with the felt pen. Make them different sizes; it's nice to have variety.

Use the paper patterns as templates and cut out leaf shapes from the pile of felted wool.

With the embroidery thread, stitch on the leaf veins.

Hand-sew some beads on to look like berries, or tiny, frosted icicles.

Hand-sew the leaves to the neck of your dress, the sleeve of your jumper, the back of your coat.

You'll need:
A *small pile of* felted wool
Beads
Embroidery thread
Needle & thread
Beading needle
Scissors
Paper
Felt pen

OR: You could sew the leaves together in a strip to make a scarf or a beautiful overgrown belt; and if you sew them together in an intricate rectangle you'll have a foliage wrap.

OR: Cut out bold shapes from the felted wool and appliqué them to a jumper. Imagine stars, picket fences, bare tree branches or hands, with the nails picked out in another colour, and hand-sew them to your winter woolly.

A TUNIC - SHAPED MINI - DRESS
inspired by DR. FRANKENSTEIN

YOU'LL NEED:
A big heap of FELTED WOOL, in a variety
    of shapes and colours
BRIGHTLY COLOURED YARN
DARNING NEEDLE

Think of your granny's crazy paving, and the mad experiments of Doctor Frankenstein and make a new garment out of snipped-up oddments of felted wool.

Blanket-stitch the edges of each oddment in a bold, bright yarn.

Sew them together into a tunic-shaped mini-dress, with minimal shaping but quite a lot of salvaged or savaged woolly material. If you are feeling more austere you can make it in plain colours, but that's not as much fun.

211

A Crocheted Jumper

EVEN IF YOU CAN'T CROCHET

When the chilly weather arrives, making something with finger-warming wool seems like a lovely idea. Armed with the *Ladybird Book of Crochet*, a hook and a hank of yarn I set about making my dream scarf – based on blankets made up of sewn-together, flower-patterned squares. It was going to be Egyptian mummy wrapping in length, but in bright colours, and not the shades of desert sands. But all I managed was this . . .

It has a certain freestyle charm that could grace the neck of a winter dress, but it's lacking in other qualities: flowers, shape, colour, a general resemblance to what most people would describe as crochet. In a seaside charity shop, I found a crocheted afghan, the size of a small field. Seam ripper in hand, I undid some of the seams to make a scarf, but there was so much more that I unanchored more squares and made them into a jumper.

212

YOU'LL NEED:

LOTS *of* CROCHET SQUARES. *Head to the charity shop: really, it is very easy to find these blankets. If that fails, commission a friend who can crochet —*
a happy hooker, I believe they're called — to go to work on your behalf
WOOL *to rejoin the squares*
A SEAM RIPPER
A DARNING NEEDLE

Carefully unpick a pile of squares from the blanket. It's best to do this under a very bright light, so that you only undo the seams and don't start unravelling the crochet as well, ahem.

Lay the squares on the floor to work out how big you want your tunic-shaped jumper, and which colours look nicest aligned up against each other.

Thread the darning needle with the matching or contrasting wool and reconfigure the squares into their new order of being.

Make a matching scarf.

A padded CAMERA BAG (with side pockets)

GUEST STAR Alison Wonderland is a photographer (look at her lovely website), and has many a camera. Even if you do not own a camera, her camera bag would be a grand thing to make. It uses photographic images of an old camera to create a bag that looks just like a vintage camera. This is probably the most difficult project on the book, so for clarity's sake, it is divided into handy sections…

YOU'LL NEED:

TRANSFER PAPER *for printers (any big supermarket sells this)*
4 *pieces of* PLAIN WHITE THICKISH COTTON FABRIC 34CM X 26CM *(front and back)*
2 *pieces of* PLAIN WHITE THICKISH COTTON FABRIC 18CM X 17CM *(pockets)*
2 *pieces of* PLAIN WHITE THICKISH COTTON FABRIC 17CM X 26CM *(bottom)*
4 *pieces* PLAIN WHITE THICKISH COTTON FABRIC 32CM X 17CM *(side panels)*
Lots of PADDING/WADDING
2 *bits of* KNICKER ELASTIC, 10CM *long*

A 'LANYARD' *with* 'BREAKAWAY CLASP'
10CM *of* RIBBON
2 *long thin strips of* TOUGH BLACK FABRIC *for handles (about 40cm each, depending on the handle length you want)*
AN OLD CAMERA
A DIGITAL CAMERA *or* A MOBILE *with an inbuilt camera*
PRINTER
AN IRON
SAFETY PIN
PAPER SCISSORS

FOR THE PHOTOS & TRANSFERS

Find a nice old camera. Using your digital camera or phone, take a picture using a plain white background. Photograph the front, back and each side of the camera.

Upload your pix to a computer. The front and back image needs to be just smaller than A4, about 25cm x 18cm and the side images should be no more than 16cm x 14cm.

Using photo or print software, reverse each image so they are back to front. 'Flip horizontal' or 'mirror' are the technical terms. Press the 'HELP!' key if you are unsure.

Position the transfer paper in the printer to print on the coated side (don't print on the side with the lines on it). Print your lovely photos and then cut around the image because you don't need the unprinted bit.

Heat up your iron. Get the transfer print with the 'camera front' image on it. Place it image side down onto one piece of the 34cm x 26cm cotton fabric; make sure the picture is nice and central on the fabric. Then iron over the whole surface of the back of the transfer slowly for about 2 minutes, but keep the iron moving and press down hard.

Do the same with the image of the 'camera back' onto another piece of 34cm x 26cm of cotton fabric.

Take the two pieces of the 18cm x 17cm cotton fabric (these will be the side pockets) and iron on the transfer of the left side of the camera on one piece and the right side of the camera on the other piece.

MAKING THE BAG

Zigzag all edges of the fabric to stop it fraying.

STUFF IT

Because you don't want your camera to get bashed about, some protective padding is required. You can unstuff a cushion, or buy new wadding from the craft shop or a haberdashery department. Using the rest of the fabric and the stuffing, you're going to make five mini pillows.

Start with the pillow that's going to make the base of the bag. Layer the stuffing between two of the 32cm x 17cm pieces of the cotton fabric, just like a sandwich. You should have a piece of fabric, a layer of stuffing, and a piece of fabric. Yum, very appetising.

Pin around the edges of the sandwich, then sew close to the edge. Make sure you sew through the stuffing, too, so that it doesn't slip around.

Next up are the sides. Make two more pillow sandwiches using the 32cm x 17cm fabric pieces. Pin and sew.

In exactly the same way, make the last two pillow sandwiches for the front and the back of the bag. Make sure you use the fabric with the printed image on one side (print side out) of the sandwich and a piece of plain fabric (34cm x 26cm) on the other.
You now should have, a plain padded base, two plain padded side panels, a padded front (with camera image) and a padded back (with camera image).

Pin and sew a small hem along the top edge of the front and back pillows to tidy the scruffy edges. Do the same with the two side panels (we will be feeding elastic through these two hems).

SIDE POCKETS

Before you sew them all together, you need to

sew the pockets to the side panels. Take your two pieces of fabric with the print of the left side of the camera and the right side of the camera, fold and pin a small hem around the four sides of each piece of fabric then sew. These are now pockets that need to be fixed to the bag.

Take one of the two pillows measuring 32cm x 17cm and pin the fabric with the print of the left-hand side of the camera (image facing out) fairly central onto the pad. Sew down both sides and along the bottom leaving the top open. Take the other pillow and sew the other pocket to it in the same way.

ASSEMBLING THE BAG

Now for a little stuffed pillow assemblage. Lay the base on the table top and arrange your padded pillows around it in a cross shape (the shape of a cross, not in a grrrrr expression), so that the side panels (with pockets positioned on the correct sides) are aligned with the small edges of the base and the front and back are aligned with the longer sides.

You'll want to make sure that the zigzag edges are hidden away inside the bag, so recalling the vital alignment of all the pieces, pin the first side panel to the base of the bag, right sides together and then sew.

With the right sides together, pin and sew the camera front to the base of the bag.

Do the same with the camera back.

With the right sides together, pin and sew the other side panel to the base of the bag. To give the bag a bit of shape, the sides will be a couple of centimetres shorter than the front and back.

RUFFLES

Take one of the pieces of elastic, put the safety pin in one end and feed it through the top hem of the side panel (make sure there is a bit of elastic hanging out the other end). Remove the safety pin and sew the elastic in place. Stretch the elastic through the hem to create a ruffle, then sew the other end in place and trim the excess elastic. Repeat on the other side. You should have nice bunched up side panels now!

HANDLES

The handles should be sewn securely to the front and back of the bag. Pin the ends of the strap (about 4cm of it) to each side of the picture on the front of the bag. Sew a small rectangle to secure the strap to the bag and then a big cross from corner to corner for added strength. Repeat on the back.

SHUT UP

The claspy bit of a 'lanyard' is the perfect device to shut your bag. Cut away most of the ribbon from the lanyard, leaving about 3cm on each side of the clasp to attach it to the bag. Leave the clasp shut for now. Get your bag and find the centre point along the top edge, between the two sides of the handle, this is where your clasp goes. Position the clasp by pinning the ribbon just inside the bag, and then do the same to the opposite side. Open the clasp and sew each side to the bag.

EPiLogue

A SWEET PEA DRESS

YOU'LL NEED:

1 READY-MADE DRESS *in* STURDY COTTON, *with a no-nonsense shape*

1 RECTANGLE *of* STURDY CANVAS *or* COTTON, *slightly wider than the dress, and at least triple the height of the seedling pots.*

SEEDLING FLOWERPOTS

COMPOST

SCENTED SWEET PEA SEEDS

WATER

SUNSHINE

RIBBON

NEEDLE AND THREAD

GARDEN TWINE

WISHFUL THINKING

Fill the little seed pots with compost

Pop a scented sweet pea seed into each pot. I'd use scented sweet peas, because they smell so lovely, and what could be better than having a sweet smelling bouquet curling around your collar? But for a really dramatic garden dress choose the non-scented giant variety of the plant – they grow at a ballistic rate.

Water the seeds.

Zigzag the edges of the sturdy cotton or canvas to prevent fraying.

Fold one third of the fabric up, wrong sides together, to make a pocket. Sew up the sides.

Sew little pockets into the bigger pocket, just bigger than the seedling pots. It's simple – stitch a row of stitches from the top of the pocket down to the bottom of the fabric, through the two layers of fabric.

Sew the big pocket to the bottom of your dress.

Pop the seedling pots into the little pockets on the bigger pocket, which is now neatly sewn onto your hardy perennial frock.

Leave outside in the rain and sunshine. Add a few drops of plant food to help the sweet peas reach their maximum growing potential.

As they grow, you may need to tie the fronds to your frock so that they grow upward, rather than trailing along the ground. Make little ribbon loops and sew them to the frock. Gently tie the fronds to the ribbon loops with the garden twine.

Wear the sweet smelling dress in the bright sunshine. Don't be startled, as spring passes and the end of the summer appears, by the sound of small explosions. It is the seedpods corkscrewing tightly and catapulting the seeds onto new terrain. Be ready to catch them for next year, and store them ready to plant for next year's growing frock.

ACKNOWLEDGMENTS

Big THANX to:

MY FAMILY: Kathleen, Una, Ciaran, Niall, Sean, Keelan, John and Lesley.

THE GUEST STARS: Amy Newman of *Gay Abandon Knickers*, Rosie Wolfenden and Harriet Vine of *Tatty Devine*, Zoë Larkins of *Love From Hetty And Dave*, Alison Withers of *AlisonWonderland*.

THE POM-POM AND SEQUIN COLLECTIVE: Chris Harvey, Gideon Defoe, Sarah and Helen O Mahoney, Elizabeth Price, Anna Small, Patrick Hargadon, Alistair O Neill, Ian Ballard, Louise Harries and Rachael Matthews of Prick Your Finger, Phil Davison of Urban Cross Stitch, Hephzibah Anderson, Sarah and Virginie of The Actionettes, Winston, Jean and Amelia Fletcher, Dora and Ivy, Fred, Beryl and Rob Pursey, Giles Borg, Gregory Webster, John Stanley, Mike Eley, Peter Grimes, Sandra and Liam Duggan, Mandy Southern, Alice Fisher, Kate Finnigan, Pam Berry.

ALL AT WEIDENFELD & NICOLSON: Laura, Sophie, Giuliana, Arzu, Rabab, Elizabeth, Mark, Jess.

And Rich Carr at Carr Design Studios.

Finally, thanks to FABRICS GALORE, charity shops and Ikea.